The Dalai Lama

My Spiritual Autobiography

Personal Reflections, Teachings and Talks

Collected by Sofia Stril-Rever
Translated by Charlotte Mandell

RIDER

Acknowledgements

We thank Caroline Parent and the Coup D'Oeil Society, who kindly authorized quotations from interviews conducted for the film *Dalaï-lama: une vie après l'autre* (*The Dalai Lama: One Life After Another*).

The photographs on pages 3 and 71 are reprinted by courtesy of the Office of the Dalai Lama. The photograph on page 161 is courtesy of Win McNamee / Getty Images and reprinted with permission. The Dalai Lama's Annual Speech to Commemorate the March 10, 1959 Lhasa Insurrection and the Kalachakra Mandala image on pages 275–280 are reproduced by courtesy of Ms. Sofia Stril-Rever and Samdhong Rinpoche.

3 5 7 9 10 8 6 4

Published in 2011 by Rider, an imprint of Ebury Publishing

Ebury Publishing is a Random House Group company

Published by arrangement with HarperOne,
an imprint of HarperCollins Publishers, New York, USA.

Copyright © 2009, 2010 by Presses de la Renaissance, Paris

Translation copyright © 2010 by Charlotte Mandell

The Random House Group Limited Reg. No. 954009

Addresses for companies within the Random House Group can be found at:
www.randomhouse.co.uk

A CIP catalogue record for this book is available from the British Library

The Random House Group Limited supports The Forest Stewardship Council (FSC®), the leading international forest certification organisation. Our books carrying the FSC label are printed on FSC® certified paper. FSC is the only forest certification scheme endorsed by the leading environmental organisations, including Greenpeace. Our paper procurement policy can be found at www.randomhouse.co.uk/environment

MIX
Paper from
responsible sources
FSC® C016897

Printed and bound in Great Britain by Clays Ltd, St Ives PLC

Copies are available at special rates for bulk orders. Contact the sales development team on 020 7840 8487 for more information.

To buy books by your favourite authors and register for offers, visit www.randomhouse.co.uk

Editor's Note

When this book was originally published in French, the Dalai Lama approved the title as *Mon autobiographie spirituelle*, My Spiritual Autobiography. In his own words, the Dalai Lama charts his spiritual journey from his boyhood days in rural Tibet, to his years as a monk in the capital city of Dharamsala, to his life in exile as a world leader. However, it might be misleading not to acknowledge the enormous contribution of his translator, Sofia Stril-Rever. Through personal interviews and archival research, Ms. Stril-Rever has expertly interwoven the Dalai Lama's personal reflections, Dharma talks, and public speeches (adding some of her own insights and useful historical background—in italics) to create a linear presentation of His Holiness's inspiring stories, lessons and spiritual truths, thus creating an accurate and approved presentation of his spiritual journey through a most remarkable life.

CONTENTS

Part Two: As a Buddhist Monk

3. Transforming Oneself   73

My Ideal: The Bodhisattva   75

Temples of Kindness in Our Hearts   82

Transforming Our Minds   88

Part Three: As the Dalai Lama

Listening to the Dalai Lama's Appeal to the World

The Dalai Lama is fourteenth in a lineage of reincarnations that came into being with the first emanation of enlightened compassion, Gendun Drup, in 1391.[1] The Dalai Lama discusses the anecdotes and accomplishments of his previous lives as naturally as he relates his childhood memories. He maintains a living link with his thirteen predecessors, often mentioning their beloved, familiar presence. He is seventy-four years old, but since he took on the burden of spiritual and temporal leadership of Tibet, his awareness encompasses seven centuries of history. In this book we meet the Dalai Lama at a time when he is reflecting on his next incarnation, for he knows that his present existence is drawing to an end. But he also knows that his life will not stop with death.

He asserts, however, that he is "no one special" but "a human being" like everyone else. Meeting him calls many certainties into question, for his "human" dimension does not exhibit the ordinary limits of our condition; I have often wondered whether the essential teaching we receive from him is simply about becoming *fully* human.

I asked myself this question again on March 10, 2006, in Dharamsala, as I listened to the speech the Dalai Lama was giving to commemorate the Lhasa insurrection. I had the feeling that his words carried far beyond the cloud-wrapped mountains and the hundreds of people gathered in a cold, steady rain to hear him. He called for human rights to be respected in Tibet, but the range of his words was universal. It was *our* humanity he was defending against a barbarism that dehumanizes it. The Dalai Lama was appealing to the world's conscience.

For fifteen years, I had followed and translated his teachings on the meditation system of the Kalachakra (the Wheel of Time), regarded as supreme by Tibetan Buddhists and dedicated to world peace. That day I saw a profoundly coherent connection between his formidable humanity, his words as a master of the Wheel of Time, and his political discourse. Thinking back on this, I understood that to be human means for him to live a spirituality that comes from the heart and is spontaneously manifested in his everyday life, as in his exchanges with world-famous scientists or his declarations in international forums. It is certainly not by chance that His Holiness the Fourteenth Dalai Lama has adopted a policy called "the Middle Way" toward China, since the Middle Way represents, in Buddhism, the essence of the wisdom that perceives emptiness.

I realized that with such an approach to spirituality, one could break down the barriers that usually compartmentalize activities, thoughts, and feelings and reach the universality of the heart. And when I agreed to let these barriers fall, I had an experience of transparency and internal conversion. I understood that, for the Dalai Lama, prayer goes beyond forms of belief. To pray starting from what is universal to all religions invites us to discover the internal dimension of our humanity and to reclaim our "human-ness."

I discussed this at length with Samdhong Rinpoche, prime minister of the Tibetan government in exile and companion in exile of the Dalai Lama; I had met him when I was studying in India at the Tibetan University of Sarnath, of which he was rector. I suggested that I bear witness to this "open" spirituality of the Dalai Lama by publishing a selection of texts that had not previously been published in French, including his March 10 speech and his speeches given in the international arena. This publication would show the impact of the Dalai Lama's *humanity* on our world at a critical time in history when the survival of future generations seems threatened. His declarations, calling for a spiritual revolution that is also an ethical revolution, urge us to acknowledge that humanity is *one*, in conformity with the Buddhist principle of interdependence. The awareness that everything is connected in the participatory reality of life is expressed on the individual level by compassion and on the collective level by universal responsibility. These notions have contributed to renewing the terminology and forging the spirit of recent United Nations texts dedicated to a culture of peace.

After the Dalai Lama agreed to the general outline of my work, which at first was titled *An Appeal to the World*, I devoted myself to it, and in the course of my research a second form of coherence struck me: that of the temporal continuity of the Dalai Lama's thinking. Indeed, although over the years his statements have been supported with new references and linked to current events and to the developments of contemporary society, analysis of those statements has followed a current that leads us back to the same source—a seemingly inexhaustible wisdom and kindness and a truth that is unfailing.

I had a striking experience of this in February 2008, at the end of our long interview for the film *The Dalai-Lama, One Life After Another.*[2] When Lhasa and Tibet flared up a month later, there was a moment of doubt. During its showing, which was planned for August, wouldn't the film be seen as out of step with current events? But very quickly it became clear that both before and after these events, the Dalai Lama's commitment to nonviolence, reconciliation, and dialogue remained unchanged. I came to the conclusion that his words have a pertinence that does not fluctuate with the events of history. His truth possesses the rare quality of constancy.

I asked myself why this was. The reason seemed to me to be that the Dalai Lama's vision embraces universal life, in perfect reciprocity. Those who reach this level of truth—called *satyagraha* by the Mahatma Gandhi, another great figure of humanity and one dear to the Dalai Lama—oppositions no longer antagonize each other but join together in harmonious complementarity. Thus, the Chinese, for instance, are not "enemies" but "brothers and sisters." My challenge was to make such profundity perceptible in the structure of the book.

In the last phase of my work I realized that the first-person texts I had selected made up a *spiritual autobiography*. I use the term "spiritual" here in the sense that the Dalai Lama gives it—namely, the full blossoming of human values that is essential for the good of all. I spoke to Samdhong Rinpoche about this idea in December 2008, during a stay in Dharamsala. When the Dalai Lama became aware of it in early January 2009, he approved of it, saying that he was very happy with the concept. He found that his statements as presented in this book articulate his fundamental aspirations, and he also authorized the publication of the facsimile of his speech on March 10, 2007, annotated with his handwritten notes and preserved by Samdhong Rinpoche.

I understood from this confirmation that I had met the challenge I set in writing this book—the challenge of making it come *alive* and bringing the reader close enough to the words of the Dalai Lama to hear them and meditate on them in an invigorating heart-to-heart dialogue from which hope can shine forth.

—Sofia Stril-Rever
  Sarnath, January 2009

My
Spiritual
Autobiography

My Three
Commitments
in Life

My first commitment in life, as a *human being,* is the promotion of human values and those qualities of spirit that are key elements in a happy life, whether of an individual, a family, or a community. These days it seems to me that we don't cultivate these inner qualities enough; that is why my priority is to develop them.

My second commitment in life, as a *Buddhist monk,* is the promotion of harmony among the different religions. In democracy we admit the necessity of pluralism in political life. But we hesitate when it's a matter of the diversity of beliefs and religions. Despite their different concepts and philosophies, all the chief religious traditions bring us the same message of love, compassion, tolerance, temperance, and self-discipline. They also have in common their potential to help us lead a happier life.

My third commitment in life, as the *Dalai Lama,* is the cause of Tibet, which concerns me very particularly. I have a special responsibility to the Tibetan people, for they continue to place their hope and confidence in me during this critical period of our history. The well-being of Tibetans is my constant motivation, and in their struggle for justice I consider myself their free spokesperson in exile.

This last commitment will come to an end as soon as a mutually satisfying solution is found between the Tibetans and the Chinese. As for the first two commitments, I will maintain them until my final breath.[1]

PART ONE

As a Human Being

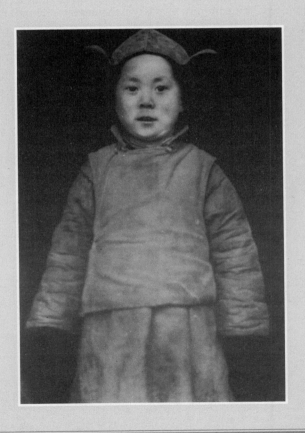

Our Common
Humanity

I Am No One Special

I am just a human being

THE TERM "DALAI LAMA" takes on different meanings according to different people. For some, this term signifies that I am a living Buddha, the earthly manifestation of Avalokiteshvara, the Bodhisattva of Compassion. For others, it means that I am a "god-king." At the end of the 1950s, to be the Dalai Lama meant fulfilling the function of "Vice President of the Steering Committee of the People's National Congress of the People's Republic of China." Then, in the beginning of the exile that followed my escape, I was called a "counter-revolutionary" and a "parasite." But none of these designations correspond to me.

As I see it, the title "Dalai Lama" represents the responsibility that has come down to me. As for me, I am just a human being, and it just so happens that I am also a Tibetan who has chosen to be a Buddhist monk. So before I narrate the events of my own spiritual journey, I would like to reflect upon what binds us all together, the essential elements of our common humanity and the compassion it calls for.

In our blood,
a vital need for affection

OUR LIFE DEPENDS ON OTHERS so much that at the root of our existence there is a fundamental need for love. That is why it is good to cultivate an authentic sense of our responsibility and a sincere concern for the welfare of others.

What is our true nature as human beings? We are not just material beings, and it is a mistake to place all our hopes for happiness in external development. Without going into the controversial debate over the creation and evolution of our universe, we all agree that each person is the product of his parents. For the most part, our conception involved not only the sexual desire of our parents but also their decision to have a child. Their plan was based on altruistic responsibility and the commitment to take care of us until we became independent. So from the very instant of our conception, our parents' love was an essential factor.

Moreover, we depended entirely on our mother's care in the beginning of our life. According to some scientists, the state of mind—calm or agitated—of a pregnant woman has an immediate physical impact on the child she is carrying.

The expression of love is also essential at birth. Since our first gesture was to suck milk from our mother's breast, we instinctively feel closer to our mother, who must also feel love in order to feed us, for if she is angry or unhappy, her milk will not flow so freely.

Then there is the critical period of formation of the brain, from birth until the age of three or four. Affectionate physical contact is the main factor for a child's normal growth. If he is not pampered, cuddled, loved, his development will be limited and his brain will not grow to its full potential.

Since the child cannot survive without another's care, love is essential. These days many children grow up in unhappy homes. Deprived of affection, later on in life they will rarely love their parents and will often have trouble loving others. This is very sad.

A few years later, when children enter school, they need to be helped by their teachers. If a teacher doesn't limit himself to academic teaching, if he also takes on the responsibility of preparing his students for life, they will have respect for him and confidence in him. The things they learn from him will leave an indelible imprint in their minds. Conversely, subjects taught by someone who doesn't care about his students' well-being will be of only passing interest to them and will soon be forgotten.

Similarly, when a sick person is treated at the hospital by a doctor who shows him human warmth, he feels comforted. The doctor's wish to lavish the best care is therapeutic in itself, regardless of the technical details of medical procedures. On the other hand, when a doctor lacks empathy and seems unfriendly, impatient, or contemptuous, even if he is very famous, his diagnosis is correct, and he prescribes the most effective remedies, the sick person is still in distress.

In the case of an everyday conversation, when our interlocutor speaks to us with human feeling, we listen and respond with pleasure, so that the conversation becomes interesting even though it is quite ordinary. On the other hand, if someone speaks coldly or harshly, we feel annoyed and want to end the conversation quickly. From the smallest to the largest event, the affection and respect of others are vital elements.

Recently, I met a group of American scientists who said that the percentage of mental illness in their country was quite high—about

12 percent of the population. From the discussion, it emerged clearly that the main cause was not lack of material resources but a lack of affection.

One thing seems obvious. Whether or not we are aware of it, from the day we are born, the need for affection is in our very blood. I believe that no one is born without this need for love. And contrary to certain modern schools of thought, this demonstrates that human beings are not limited to the physical plane alone. No material object, no matter how beautiful or precious it is, can give us the feeling of being loved, because our deeper identity, our true character, is rooted in the subjective nature of the mind.

Compassion, what I sometimes also call human *affection,* is the determining factor of our life. Connected to the palm of the hand, the five fingers become functional; cut off from it, they are useless. Similarly, every human action becomes dangerous when it is deprived of human feeling. When they are performed with feeling and respect for human values, all activities become constructive.

My mother,
a compassionate woman

I WAS BORN OF A SIMPLE FAMILY from the remote Amdo province in Tibet. As a child, I grew up surrounded by the loving-kindness of my mother, a woman of great compassion. And after I arrived in Lhasa at the age of four, everyone around me, my teachers and the servants, taught me what it means to be good, honest, and caring. That is the environment I grew up in.

Later on, my classical education in Buddhist thought exposed me to concepts such as interdependence and the human potential for infinite compassion. That allowed me to become aware of the importance of universal responsibility, nonviolence, and understanding among religions. Today faith in these values gives me a powerful motivation to promote basic human qualities. In the context of my own struggle for human rights and a greater freedom of the Tibetan people, these values continue to guide my commitment to the nonviolent path.[1]

It's time to think in
human terms

WHEN I SPEAK OF KINDNESS and compassion, I am not expressing myself as a Buddhist, or as the Dalai Lama, or as a Tibetan, but rather as a human being. And I hope that you also consider yourselves as human beings, rather than as Americans, Westerners, or members of one group or another. Such distinctions are secondary. When we speak as human beings, we can touch the essential thing. If I say, "I am a monk," or, "I am a Buddhist," it's a question of realities that are temporary in comparison with my human nature. The fact of having been born *human* is fundamental and will not change until death. The rest, whether or not you are learned, rich or poor, is secondary.

Today we are confronted with many problems. Our responsibility is directly involved in conflicts provoked by ideology, religion, race, or the economy. Consequently, the time has come for us to think in *human* terms, on a deeper level where we respectfully take into consideration the equality of others, for they are human beings like us. We must construct close relationships in mutual confidence, understanding, and support, without paying attention to differences of culture, philosophy, religion, or belief.

After all, all human beings are the same—made up of flesh, bone, and blood. We all want happiness, and we all try to avoid suffering. We are the members of one single human family, and our arguments are born from secondary causes. Disputes, lies, and killings are useless.

Every person we meet is
our brother or sister

I WOULD LIKE TO STRESS THIS POINT, which I think is essential. Each person's happiness can make a profound, effective contribution that can improve the entire human community.

By realizing that we share the same need to be loved, we have the feeling that in every circumstance every person we meet is our brother or our sister. It doesn't matter if their face is unfamiliar or if their appearance and behavior are unusual. There is no significant chasm between ourselves and others. It doesn't make sense to pay attention to external differences, for our fundamental nature is identical.

In the final analysis, humanity is *one,* and our only home is this little planet. If we want to protect it, each one of us has to experience universal altruism. Only this feeling will eliminate the selfish motives that impel people to take advantage of each other. With a sincere and open heart, we are naturally confident and sure of ourselves, and we have nothing to fear from others.

I believe that at all levels of society—family, national, and international—the key to a better, happier world is greater compassion. It is not necessary to become religious, or to believe in an ideology. The important thing is to develop our human qualities as much as we can. I try to treat every person I meet like an old friend, and that gives me a real sensation of happiness.

Loving-kindness, the
condition of our survival

AT BIRTH, human beings are naturally endowed with the qualities we need for our survival, such as caring, nurturing, and loving-kindness. Despite the fact that we already possess such positive qualities, however, we tend to neglect them. As a result, humanity faces unnecessary problems. We need to make more efforts to sustain and develop these basic qualities. That is why the promotion of human values is of primary importance. We also need to focus on cultivating good human relations since, whatever our differences of nationality, religious faith, race, wealth, or education, we are all human beings. Faced with difficulties, we always meet someone, a stranger perhaps, who spontaneously offers us help. We all depend on each other in difficult circumstances, and we do so unconditionally. We don't ask who people are before we help them. We help them because they are human beings like us.[2]

I pray for a more loving
human family

Even when I meet a stranger
Each time I have the same feeling:
"He is another member of my human family."
Such an attitude deepens
My affection and respect for all beings.
May this natural loving-kindness
Become my small contribution to world peace!
I pray for a world that is more friendly,
More loving, and for a better understanding
Among the human family, on this planet.
That is the appeal I make from the bottom of my heart
To all those who hate suffering
And cherish lasting happiness.

We are all alike

No matter what part of the world we come from, fundamentally we are all the same human beings. We all seek happiness and want to avoid suffering. We all have essentially the same needs and similar concerns. As human beings, we all want to be free, to have the right to decide our own destiny as individuals as well as the destiny of our people. That is human nature.

The problems that confront us today are created by man, whether they are violent conflicts, destruction of the environment, poverty, or hunger. These problems can be resolved thanks to human efforts, by understanding that we are brothers and sisters and by developing this sense of fraternity. We must cultivate a universal responsibility toward each other and extend it to the planet that we have to share.

I feel optimistic that the ancient values that have sustained mankind are reaffirming themselves today, preparing the way for a better, happier twenty-first century.

I pray for all of us, oppressor and friend, so that together we can succeed in building a better world through mutual understanding and love, and that in doing so we may reduce the pain and suffering of all sentient beings.[3]

On December 10, 1989, the Dalai Lama's Nobel Peace Prize acceptance speech, quoted in part above, was broadcast throughout the world. The cause of Tibet had become international. But it was not as the leader of a government in exile, or as a Tibetan, that the Dalai Lama accepted the Nobel Prize. He shared this distinction as a human being with all those who recognize each other's basic human values. By claiming his humanity in the universal language of the heart, which goes beyond ideological rifts and notions of cultural identity, the Dalai Lama gave us back our humanity.

In Oslo on December 10, 1989, we all received the Nobel Peace Prize.

Until My Last Breath, I Will Practice Compassion

What do we mean by "compassion"?

COMPASSION CAN BE A MIXTURE of desire and attachment; the love of parents for their child, for instance, is often associated with their own emotional needs and so is not wholly compassionate. Similarly, in marriage the love between husband and wife—especially in the beginning, when one isn't fully aware of the other's character—is more like attachment than real love. Our desire can be so strong that the person we are attached to seems good, even if that person is actually very negative. What's more, we have a tendency to exaggerate the slightest qualities. So when one person's attitude changes, the other person is often disappointed, and his own attitude changes as a result. That is a sign that love was motivated more from personal need than from an authentic concern for the loved one. Real compassion is not just an emotional response; it is a firm, thought-out commitment. Therefore, an authentic attitude of compassion does not change, even faced with another person's negative behavior.

Of course, it is not at all easy to develop this form of compassion. To begin, we should understand that other people are human beings just like us. They want happiness and do not want to suffer. When you acknowledge that all beings are equal in their wish for happiness and their right to obtain it, you spontaneously feel an empathy that brings you closer to them. By accustoming your mind to a universal altruism, you will develop a feeling of responsibility for others and the wish to help them overcome their suffering effectively. Such a desire is not selective but is applied impartially to everyone. As long as human beings feel pleasure and pain as you do, there is no logical basis that authorizes you to establish distinctions or to diminish your solicitude for them, even when their attitude is negative.

With patience and time, you will develop this form of compassion. Of course, selfishness and attachment to the sense of an independent, autonomous self are factors that inhibit compassion. In fact, genuine compassion can be experienced only when clinging to the self is eliminated. But that should not prevent us from making a start and progressing on the path now.

True compassion is universal

WE SOMETIMES WRONGLY LIKEN compassion to a feeling of pity. We should analyze the nature of true compassion more deeply.

We naturally feel close to our friends, but that is not authentic compassion. It is a feeling that is partial, whereas true compassion is universal.

True compassion does not stem from the pleasure of feeling close to one person or another, but from the conviction that other people are just like me and want not to suffer but to be happy, and from a commitment to help them overcome what causes them to suffer. I must realize that I can help them suffer less. That is true, well thought-out compassion.

This attitude is not limited to the circle of our relatives and friends. It must extend to our enemies too. True compassion is impartial and bears with it a feeling of responsibility for the welfare and happiness of others.

True compassion brings with it the appeasement of internal tensions, a state of calmness and serenity. It turns out to be very useful in daily life when we're faced with situations that require self-confidence. And a compassionate person creates a warm, relaxed atmosphere of welcome and understanding around him. In human relations, compassion contributes to promoting peace and harmony.

The power of compassion

ANGER AND HATRED are the main obstacles to compassion. These powerful emotions have the ability to overwhelm the mind completely, but we can sometimes control them. If we don't master them, they constantly torment us, preventing us from attaining the serenity that characterizes a loving mind.

It is good to ask yourself first of all whether or not anger has any value. Sometimes, when we're overcome with discouragement and faced with a difficult situation, anger seems to bring an extra amount of energy, confidence, and determination. That is when it is good to examine our state of mind carefully. Although it is true that anger confers a certain energy, when we observe it we discover that it is blind. It is impossible to determine if its result will be positive or negative, because anger clouds the best part of the brain, reason. That is why the energy of anger should be subject to caution. It can inspire behavior that is terribly destructive and unfortunate. When it is pushed to its extreme, anger can make people crazy, to the point where they act to their own and others' detriment.

We can still develop an energy that's just as strong, but much better controlled than anger, in order to confront difficult circumstances. This controlled energy comes both from a compassionate attitude and from reason, combined with patience. These are very effective antidotes against anger. Unfortunately, many people scorn these qualities, likening them to weakness. I believe, on the contrary, that they are the true signs of inner strength. Compassion is by nature kind, peaceful, and gentle, while still being very powerful. People who easily lose their patience are uncertain and unstable. That is why in my opinion an outburst of anger is an infallible sign of weakness.

Faced with a problem, then, try to remain humble, while keeping a sincere attitude, and think about the right solution. No doubt some people will try to take advantage of your attitude. If your calm seems to encourage unfair aggression, be firm, but with compassion. If it turns out to be necessary for you to prove your point by severe countermeasures, do so without resentment or bad intentions.

You must understand that even if your adversaries seem to be harming you, in the end their destructive activity will turn against them. To rein in your selfish impulse to retaliate, remember your desire to practice compassion and your responsibility to help others avoid suffering the consequences of their own actions. Calmly chosen measures will be more effective, better adapted, and more powerful, whereas retaliation based on the blind energy of anger rarely reaches its goal.

I am a professional laugher

I HAVE BEEN CONFRONTED WITH many difficult circumstances throughout the course of my life, and my country is going through a critical period. But I laugh often, and my laughter is contagious. When people ask me how I find the strength to laugh now, I reply that I am a professional laugher. Laughing is a characteristic of the Tibetans, who are different in this from the Japanese or the Indians. They are very cheerful, like the Italians, rather than a little reserved, like the Germans or the English.

My cheerfulness also comes from my family. I come from a small village, not a big city, and our way of life is more jovial. We are always amusing ourselves, teasing each other, joking. It's our habit.

To that is added, as I often say, the responsibility of being realistic. Of course problems are there. But thinking only of the negative aspect doesn't help to find solutions, and it destroys peace of mind. Everything, though, is relative. You can see the positive side of even the worst of tragedies if you adopt a holistic perspective. If you take the negative as absolute and definitive, however, you increase your worries and anxiety, whereas by broadening the way you look at a problem, you understand what is bad about it, but you accept it. This attitude comes to me, I think, from my practice and from Buddhist philosophy, which help me enormously.

Take the loss of our country, for example. We are a stateless people, and we must confront adversity along with many painful circumstances in Tibet itself. Nevertheless, such experiences also bring many benefits.

As for me, I have been homeless for half a century. But I have found a large number of new homes throughout the vast world. If I had remained at the Potala, I don't think I would have had the chance to meet so many personalities, so many heads of state in Asia, Taiwan, the United States, and Europe, popes as well as many famous scientists and economists.

The life of exile is an unfortunate life, but I have always tried to cultivate a happy state of mind, appreciating the opportunities this existence without a settled home, far from all protocol, has offered me. This way I have been able to preserve my inner peace.[4]

I am a devoted servant
of compassion

THE PRACTICE OF COMPASSION gives me the greatest satisfaction. Whatever the circumstances, whatever tragedy I am faced with, I practice compassion. That reinforces my inner strength and brings me happiness by giving me the feeling that my life is useful. Up until now, I have tried to practice compassion as well as I can, and I will continue to do so until my last day, until my last breath. For in the deepest part of my being, I feel that I am a devoted servant of compassion.

———————

The Dalai Lama has often said that when he left Tibet he left all his wealth behind him, but he carried in his heart the priceless treasure of infinite compassion.

Compassion,
path of my happiness

A BIG QUESTION UNDERLIES OUR EXPERIENCE, whether or not we are aware of it: What is the meaning of life? I have thought about this, and I would like to share my thoughts on this subject.

I believe that the aim of life is to be happy. From birth, every human being aspires to happiness and does not want to suffer. Social conditions, education, and ideology do not affect these tendencies of our deepest being. That is why it is important to find out what will bring us the most happiness.

First, we divide happiness and suffering into two main categories, mental and physical. But it is the mind that exercises the most influence over us. Unless we are seriously ill or deprived of necessities, our physical condition plays a secondary role in life. When the body is satisfied, we're almost not aware of it. The mind, on the other hand, registers the slightest event, no matter how minor it is. So we must devote our efforts to developing peace of mind.

According to my own experience, the highest level of inner calm comes from the development of love and compassion. The more concerned we are with the happiness of others, the more we increase our own well-being. Friendliness and warmth toward others relax mental tensions and help us to dissipate fears or insecurity so that we can overcome obstacles. That is the ultimate source of success in life.

In this world, where we are bound to encounter difficulties, if we lose hope and become discouraged, we reduce our ability to face things. What's more, if we remember that everyone, not just ourselves, has to experience suffering, this realistic perspective reinforces our determination and our ability to overcome difficulty. In fact, with this attitude, every new obstacle will be regarded as a good opportunity to improve our state of mind!

That is how we can gradually strive for more compassion—by cultivating both real sympathy when faced with the suffering of others and a desire to help them free themselves of it. In this way our own serenity and inner strength will increase.

I love the smile,
unique to humans

IF WE ARE CONTENT just to think that compassion, rationality, and patience are good, that is not actually enough to develop these qualities. Difficulties provide the occasion to put them into practice. Who can make such occasions arise? Certainly not our friends, but rather our enemies, for they are the ones who pose the most problems. So that if we truly want to progress on the path, we must regard our enemies as our best teachers.

For whoever holds love and compassion in high esteem, the practice of tolerance is essential, and it requires an enemy. We must be grateful to our enemies, then, because they help us best engender a serene mind! Anger and hatred are the real enemies that we must confront and defeat, not the "enemies" who appear from time to time in our lives.

Of course it is natural and right that we all want to have friends. I often say jokingly that a truly selfish person must be altruistic! You have to take care of others, of their well-being, by helping them and serving them, to have even more friends and make more smiles blossom. The result? When you yourself need help, you will find all you need! On the other hand, if you neglect others' happiness, you will be the loser in the long run. Is friendship born of arguments, anger, jealousy, and unbridled competition? I don't think so. Only affection produces authentic friends.

In contemporary materialistic society, if you have money and power, you have the impression of having a lot of friends. But they aren't your friends; they are the friends of your money and power. If you lose your wealth and influence, you will have trouble finding those people again.

Unfortunately, so long as things are going well, we think we can get along all by ourselves. However, as our situation and health decline, we soon realize how wrong we were. That is when we understand who really helps us. To prepare ourselves for such a time, by making true friends who are useful when we need them most, we must cultivate altruism.

As for me, I always want more friends. I love smiles, and my wish is to see more smiles, real smiles, for there are many kinds—sarcastic, artificial, or diplomatic. Some smiles don't arouse any satisfaction, and some even engender suspicion or fear. An authentic smile, though, arouses an authentic feeling of freshness, and I think the smile belongs only to human beings. If we want those smiles, we must create the reasons that make them appear.

2

My Lives Without Beginning or End

In Dharamsala, among the Tibetans in exile, we go to meet this human being, so fully human that just approaching him can change our lives. That is the experience related by the renowned psychologist Paul Ekman: as he shook the Dalai Lama's hand, he says he had the feeling he was "touching" compassion. He discovered that kindness can be "palpable," and his life was transformed by this experience.[5] Ekman's personal history, marked by the suffering of a difficult childhood, equipped him with feelings of anger and resentment. After meeting the Dalai Lama, he found the strength to forgive and never to give way to anger again. Having become another man, he wondered about this metamorphosis. He came to the conclusion that the Dalai Lama could make others better because in the course of his daily meditations he had so completely bathed his mind in love and compassion that he was able to transmit these qualities directly to another person.

To meet Tenzin Gyatso, His Holiness the Fourteenth Dalai Lama, we go to the Indian state of Himachal Pradesh. Called also "the Land of the

Gods," this region in northwest India stretches to the foot of the Himalayan barrier, whose snow-covered peaks rise in stages above the Kangra plain. Kangra was once a city of maharajas and a crossroads of Indian cultures—Moghul, Sikh, then British, and finally Tibetan.

Geographically we are in India, but spiritually we are in Tibetan territory. At regular intervals, the valley resounds with the deep call of Tibetan ritual instruments: radongs, gyalings, and kanglings. From these instruments, which used to be made from the bones of a young Brahman, the monks of the Roof of the World draw grave, haunting sounds that open the mind to the dimension of the sacred. Prayer is omnipresent, murmured by the pilgrims fingering their rosaries, engraved on the walls of houses, printed in black ink on squares of cloth dyed the colors of the four elements and tied to poles. The wind blows through the holy syllables and carries them far and wide, spreading their blessings over all beings it touches.

The Dalai Lama's residence is built atop a hill overlooking McLeod Ganj. This hill station, named after a Scottish governor of the Punjab, used to be the summer lodgings for officers of the British Raj; today it has become "little Lhasa." It is home to about ten thousand people—one-quarter of them monks and nuns—who live in monasteries that are painted ochre or burgundy and stacked on the high foothills of the Dhauladhar range. Many hotels dot the area, since people from all over the world come to visit this hamlet with its steep little streets; they come for the teachings that the Dalai Lama gives during the Great Monlam, the festival of aspiration prayers that begins in Lhasa in the first month of the Tibetan year. The tradition has continued in exile, attracting not just visitors from Tibet but also Europeans, Australians, and Americans by the hundreds. They come as either followers of the Buddhist path or curious onlookers, and with them come Asians from Japan, Korea, Thailand, Vietnam, Malaysia, Singapore, Hong Kong, and Taiwan. With the revival of monastic vows in Mongolia and the former

Soviet republics of Kalmykia, Buriatia, and Tuva, groups from Central Asia have also come for over a dozen years now to pay homage to the Dalai Lama.

Above a residence surrounded by oaks, spruce, and Himalayan cedars with slim, proud silhouettes, white eagles with golden beaks wheel, along with kites and other raptors. Birds soar upward in pairs, an eagle and a crow flying together, outlining quick arcs in the sky, ascending and descending at dizzying speeds.

It is February 2008, just before the Tibetan New Year, Losar, the first day of the lunar year. Early in the morning, costumed monks perform cham, the dance ritual intended to chase away the negativities of the past year and ward off evil spirits. The Dalai Lama, in retreat, has granted only a few interviews. A group of Mongolians are crowded around his doorway in ceremonial robes woven in silk brocade with silver ornaments.

Historically, this fierce people defended the Dalai Lamas against Manchu incursions; the Khans had vowed to protect the sovereign of the Roof of the World, whom they venerated as their spiritual leader. In Mongolia today Buddhism has been reborn, and temples that were destroyed throughout the decades of communism have been rebuilt. But only one-fifth of the population of Mongolia are Mongols—the majority are Chinese. This is the situation that the Dalai Lama dreads for his country. Tibet is in fact undergoing demographic aggression by Han Chinese and a forced sinicization of the culture.

The Mongolians have taken their leave, their eyes wet with tears, after offering the spiritual leader a kata, or ceremonial scarf, this one made of blue silk and embroidered with the eight auspicious symbols. The Dalai Lama's private secretary, Tenzin Taklha, summons me as His Holiness, with a gesture of his hand, invites me to join him without any further ado in the interview room. The large bay windows invite the sky's infinity into the long, soberly furnished room, its walls covered in thangkas, paintings on cloth representing the great compassionate figures of Enlightenment.

When the Dalai Lama talks about himself in private, it is with the same jovial, spontaneous simplicity as on the international stage. His infectious cheerfulness can very quickly give way to sadness when the world's sufferings are mentioned: "Many Buddhas have come among us, and yet humanity continues to suffer. That is the reality of samsara. It is not the failure of the Buddhas, but of human beings, who have not put the teachings into practice."

I Rejoice at Being the Son of Simple Farmers

My everyday life

M Y DAYS BEGIN at around three or three-thirty in the morning. When I wake up, I think of the Buddha, and I recite a prayer of salutation written by the great Indian sage Nagarjuna. I say my prayer lying down, my hands joined, half-respectful, half-asleep. . . .

As a practicing Buddhist monk, as soon as I wake up I pay homage to the Buddha, and I try to prepare my mind to be more altruistic, more compassionate, during the day to come so that I can be of benefit to beings. Then I do physical exercise—I walk on a treadmill.

Around five o'clock I have breakfast; then I have a few more meditation sessions, and I recite prayers until about eight or nine. Afterward I usually read the paper, but sometimes I also go to the interview room for meetings. If I have nothing else to do, I mainly study the Buddhist scriptures that my teachers have taught me in the past, but I also read some recent books.

Then I practice analytic meditation on altruism, which we call *bodhicitta,* or "enlightened mind," in Buddhist terminology. I also meditate on emptiness. Bodhicitta and emptiness are the most important meditations in my daily practice, for they help me throughout the entire day. Whatever difficulties, sad events, or bad news may come up, these meditations allow me to stabilize my mind profoundly and support it from within.

After lunch I go back to the interview room for other meetings. At this time [Tibetan New Year], almost every week, I receive Tibetans who have recently arrived from Tibet.

Around five o'clock it's time for my evening tea. As a Buddhist monk, I don't eat dinner. If I'm hungry, I snack on a cookie, asking the Buddhas for forgiveness. Then I devote myself to more prayers and meditations. . . .

Around seven or eight o'clock I go to sleep—not without examining what I did during the day first! Some nights I sleep eight or even nine hours. That's the best time! Total relaxation . . . (*Laughs.*)

I was born on the fifth day
of the fifth month . . .

I WAS BORN on the fifth day of the fifth month in the Wood Pig year according to the Tibetan calendar, or July 6, 1935, in the Western calendar. I was given the name Lhamo Thondup, which means, literally, "Goddess who accomplishes all wishes." Tibetan names for people, places, and things often sound picturesque when they're translated. Tsangpo, for instance, the name of one of the largest rivers in Tibet—which in India becomes the powerful Brahmaputra—means "the Purifier."

The name of my village is Takster, or "Roaring Tiger." When I was a child, it was a poor little commune, built on a hill overlooking a wide valley. The grazing land was used not by farmers but by nomads, because of the unpredictable weather in the region. When I was little, my family, along with about twenty others, earned a meager living from this land.

Takster is situated in the extreme northeastern part of the country, in the province of Amdo. The house where I was born was typical of that part of Tibet—built of stone and earth, with a flat roof. The gutters, made from juniper branches hollowed out to channel rainwater, were the only unusual element of its architecture. Right in front of the house, between its two "arms" or wings, was a little courtyard with, in the center, a tall pole to which a flag printed with many prayers was attached.

Animals were housed behind the house, which had six rooms: the kitchen, where we spent most of our time during the winter; the shrine room with a little altar, where we all gathered for the morning offerings; my parents' bedroom; a guest room; a storage room for our provisions; and finally, a stable for the animals.

Children didn't have a room of their own. As a baby, I slept with my mother, and then in the kitchen, near the stove. We had neither chairs nor beds, properly speaking, but there were raised wooden platforms to sleep on in my parents' room and in the guest bedroom. We also had a few wooden hutches, painted in bright colors.

I can see into the humblest souls

MY FAMILY LIVED in a very remote region. Sining, the capital of Amdo, was the closest town, but it took three hours by horse or mule to get there. Our village was very poor, and it's only thanks to my older brother, who was recognized when he was very young as a reincarnate lama from the great monastery of Kumbum, that we had a little more than other people.

I have always rejoiced in my modest origins. If I had been born in a rich or aristocratic family, it would have been hard for me to share the concerns of the simple people of Tibet. Those years of my early childhood in Takster had a profound effect on me. They allow me to see into the humblest souls, to sympathize with them, as I try to make their living conditions better.

I had many brothers and sisters; my mother brought sixteen children into the world, only seven of whom survived. It was my older sister who helped my mother in childbirth when I was born, since she was already eighteen. We were very close, and there were many joys in that harsh life.

My parents were small-scale farmers but not, strictly speaking, peasants, since they rented a plot of land and tilled it themselves. Barley and buckwheat are the main grains of Tibet. My family grew them, along with potatoes. But many times all the year's efforts were ruined by strong hailstorms or drought.

We also had a few animals, which were a more reliable source of income. I remember our five or six *dzomos,* which my mother used to milk.[6] As soon as I was able to stand on my feet I would go with her to the stable. In the folds of my robe I would carry a bowl, and she would pour milk, still warm, straight into it.

We also had a herd of about eighty head of livestock, both sheep and goats, and my father almost always had one or two horses, sometimes three, to which he was very attached. In the region, he had the reputation of knowing how to take care of horses and even curing them on occasion.

Finally, my family raised two yaks, which are a gift of nature to mankind, since they can survive at an altitude of over ten thousand feet. We also kept hens for their eggs, which I was in charge of gathering from the chicken coop. I often amused myself by climbing up to the nest-box, where I liked to perch and cluck like a hen!

My parents never thought I might be the Fourteenth Dalai Lama

IT WAS MY MOTHER who reminded me of the memories of the first two years of my life. She was surprised to hear me repeating at a very early age: "I come from central Tibet. I have to go back there! I will take you all with me." And my favorite game was packing my bags; then I would say good-bye to everyone and pretend to leave, sitting astride improvised mounts. My relatives thought they were children's games, and no one really paid any attention to them. Only later on did my mother think that I had an intuition of the fate that lay in store for me.

Truthfully, my parents never suspected that I might be the Fourteenth Dalai Lama. Several months before I was born, my father had suffered a strange illness, losing consciousness many times and with repeated bouts of vertigo, until he finally had to take to his bed and leave all the household work to my pregnant mother. Curiously, on the morning of my birth he felt cured, got up in full form, and said his prayers, as if he had never been sick. When he learned that a son had been born at dawn on this lucky day, he said to my mother that this child was probably not like the others, and that he should become a monk.

I recognize *my* rosary

I STILL WONDER TO THIS DAY how the search party for the Fourteenth Dalai Lama discovered our little village so far from everything, lost in the great grass plains of Amdo.

In 1933 my predecessor, Thubten Gyatso, had left this world at the age of fifty-seven. His body was embalmed, according to custom, and the monks were startled to discover one morning that his head, which had been facing south, had turned to the northeast. This unusual movement was interpreted as a sure sign pointing toward the region of his next reincarnation.

Soon after, a vision of the regent's confirmed this sign. On the sacred water of Lhamo Lhatso, he had seen the Tibetan letters *Ah*, *Ka*, and *Ma* glittering. Then there had formed the image of a monastery with three floors, with a turquoise and gold roof, and then a little house appeared. It had gutters with knotted, unusual shapes. There was no doubt for the regent that the letter *Ah* designated the province of Amdo, toward which my late predecessor had turned his head after his death. *Ka* seemed logically to represent the initial of the monastery of Kumbum, with its three floors and turquoise roof. They still had to identify the little house with the strange gutters.

When the search mission saw, in the valley, the twisting juniper branches that ran beneath the roof of the family farm, it was clear to everyone that the new Dalai Lama was living here. And when, after investigation, they learned that a boy had been born in this house, the members of the group decided to present themselves at our door and ask for hospitality for the night.

The lama who was guiding the delegation passed himself off as a servant and headed for the kitchen. I ran over to him, sat down on his lap, and demanded the rosary he was carrying, asserting that it was my own. This familiarity earned me the reproaches of my mother, but the lama offered to give me the rosary if I was able to say his name. I replied without hesitating: "You are Sera Aga," which, in local dialect, meant: "You are the lama of Sera." I also called his companions by their names and spent the rest of the evening playing with him, until it was time for bed. The next morning the group went back to Lhasa, without saying anything to my parents.

I successfully pass the tests of
remembering my previous life

THREE WEEKS LATER, a full delegation of lamas and religious dignitaries came to visit us again. This time they brought several personal objects that had belonged to my predecessor, mixed up with others that had no connection to him. It has been shown that young reincarnate children remember objects and people from their past life or are able to recite texts from the Sutras even before they have learned them.

When they showed me two canes, I touched one hesitantly, looked at it a few more seconds, then seized the other one, which had belonged to the Great Thirteenth. Then I lightly tapped the arm of the lama who was staring at me, asserting that this cane belonged to me and reproaching him for having taken it from me.

Likewise I recognized, among several identical black and yellow rosaries, the ones that belonged to my predecessor. Finally, they had me choose between two drums: one was simple and small, which the previous Dalai Lama used to summon the servants; the other was larger and decorated with gold ribbons. I chose the little one, which I began pounding in the customary way for ritual practices.

These tests, which I passed successfully, persuaded the members of the delegation that they had found the reincarnation they had been looking for. It was also a good omen that the Thirteenth Dalai Lama had stayed at the neighboring monastery when he was returning from China. He had been welcomed there by a ceremony, and my father, who was nine at the time, had been present for it. The leader of the search party remembered that the Thirteenth Dalai Lama had forgotten a pair of yellow boots at the monastery, which was interpreted as a sign that he would return. He had also briefly contemplated the house where I was born and remarked that it was a very beautiful site.

My Childhood in Lhasa

I climb up onto the Lion Throne

During the winter of 1940, they brought me to the Potala, where I was officially enthroned as the spiritual leader of Tibet. I have no particular memory of this ceremony, except that, for the first time, I sat on the Lion Throne, a wooden seat, very large, encrusted with jewels and magnificently sculpted, set up in the Sishi Phuntsok, "the Hall of all the meritorious actions in the temporal and spiritual world," the main assembly hall in the eastern wing of the Potala.

Soon afterward, I was led to the Jokhang Temple, in the middle of the city, and there I was ordained a novice monk; then we proceeded to the hair-cutting ceremony, which I don't remember much of, except that at a certain moment, when I saw the brocade costumes of the monks performing a ritual dance, I shouted excitedly to my brother, "Look over there!"

My hair was symbolically cut by Reting Rinpoche, the regent, who, along with acting as head of state until I came of age, occupied the position of my chief tutor. In the beginning, I was guarded around him, but then I began to like him very much. He was a man with a great imagination and a very open mind, who always saw the bright side of life. He liked picnics and horses, which made him a great friend of my father's. Unfortunately, during his years as regent he became a controversial character in a corrupt government in which buying and selling high offices was common practice.

At the time of my ordination there were a lot of rumors to the effect that Reting Rinpoche could not carry out the hair-cutting ritual, since people were saying he had broken his vows of celibacy and was no longer a monk. Still, following the ancient custom, I exchanged my name of Lhamo Thondup for his own, Jamphel Yeshe. Attached to several other names, my full name became Jamphel ("Awakened Wisdom") Ngawang ("Prince of Speech") Lobsang ("Perfect Intelligence") Yeshe ("Exalted Wisdom") Tenzin ("Holder of the Teachings") Gyatso (Ocean [of Wisdom]").

I find *my* teeth

WHEN WE ARRIVED IN LHASA, my family and I were housed in the summer palace of the Dalai Lamas, the Norbulingka, or Jewel Park, whose gardens were overflowing with flowers. It was the eighth month of the year, and in that season the fruit trees were covered with apples, pears, and walnuts, to our great delight. But my mother remembers that I had only one idea in my head: finding a certain box in my rooms. I stated that *my* teeth were stored there, and I had all my predecessor's sealed trunks opened, one after the other, until I found what I was looking for. Seeing a box wrapped in brocade, I cried out that it contained *my* teeth. We did in fact find a set of dentures that had belonged to the Thirteenth Dalai Lama.

I had forgotten this anecdote because my mind is dominated by memories of my present existence, attached to my present body. The events of my previous life have grown vague. Unless I make an effort to bring them back to mind, I don't remember them.

Childhood memories

THE TIBETAN GOVERNMENT had built a house for my mother, and we lived apart, since I lived within the yellow walls of Norbulingka. But I would go almost every day to my mother's house. My parents also came to see me in the apartment of the Dalai Lamas, and we were very close. My mother visited me quite often, at least once a month, accompanied by my brothers and sisters.

I remember our children's games in the gardens of Norbulingka.

I also remember a temple with a stuffed leopard and a stuffed tiger. They looked so real to my younger brother, Tenzin Chögyal, that the mere sight of them filled him with terror. It didn't matter that I reassured him, saying they were just stuffed animals—he didn't dare go near them.

During the winter, at the Potala, the custom was that I should go into retreat for a month. I found myself in a room with no sun, with its windows shut, where it was cold. It was an old room (two or three hundred years old), and because of the oil lamps it looked like a kitchen—dark, smoky, dirty.

There were also rats! While we chanted or recited prayers, I could see them coming, for they liked to scurry around the *torma* offerings and drink the water in the offering bowls. . . . I couldn't tell if the deities liked this water, but I could see clearly that the rats loved it! *(Laughs.)*

All through these years, my teacher never smiled. He was always very, very severe. But during this same time, shepherds, simple people, would be passing by joyfully, with their herds of cows and other animals. Hearing them sing, I'd sometimes say to myself, "I wish I could be one of them!"

I indulge in illegal treats

I REMEMBER THE SEVERE EXPRESSION of my teacher, who often scolded me. So as soon as lessons were over, I would run to my mother's house for refuge, determined not to go back to the official residence of the Dalai Lamas. My mind was made up to remain with her, free from any obligation to study, but then, when the time came for the evening lesson, I would meekly return to my official residence. . . . *(Laughs.)*

These are all childhood stories. . . .

Memories of my life when I was little come back to me, funny anecdotes. For instance, in the Dalai Lama's kitchen, traditionally, no pork or eggs or fish were ever cooked. But my father liked pork very much. Occasionally, when I went back to my parents' place, I would ask for pork. . . . *(Laughs.)*

I remember that I would sit right next to my pork-loving father, almost like a little dog waiting for his tidbit. . . . Eggs too were a treat. Sometimes my mother cooked eggs especially for me. It was a little illegal! *(Laughs.)*

The Dalai Lama's childhood resembled an ordinary childhood and could almost have been our own. Pampered by his parents' love, he led a life filled with games that alternated with studies, breaking the rules, and boyish tricks to escape the vigilance of severe teachers.

We conceive of the Dalai Lama's ability to concentrate, his memory, and his aptitude for meditative practice as hardly ordinary, but he himself is very modest about these qualities. At the age of eighteen, when Chinese occupation was looming, he received the rank of Geshe or "Doctor of Divinity." This title requires intensive training under the strict authority of teachers, and his teachers were even more demanding than normal since they were training him for an exceptional fate. They sometimes administered punishments, "after he had prostrated and asked forgiveness, with a whip that had a gold handle, but that hurt no less than ordinary whips."

The Dalai Lama delights in relating anecdotes, punctuated by loud bursts of laughter, about his innocent pranks. He takes pleasure in presenting himself as a "clever little rascal," trying to make us believe in his innate mischievousness!

The portrait provided by Heinrich Harrer, the Dalai Lama's "professor in the secular sciences," is more complimentary and brings something else to light: "People spoke of the intelligence of this boy as miraculous. It was said that he had only to read a book to know it by heart; and it was known that he had long taken an interest in all that happened in his country and used to criticise or commend the decisions of the National Assembly."[7]

Hidden in the heart of the Himalayan Mountains, Tibetan society has remained apart from modernization and technological progress and continues its timeless rituals and religious practices. The Dalai Lama, eager to learn about the world outside, found a special interlocutor in Heinrich Harrer. The Austrian alpinist and explorer had the singular privilege, between 1949 and 1951, of instructing him in history, geography, biology, astronomy, and mechanical engineering, fields of study that completely opened up new horizons of knowledge for the teenager.

Harrer left Tibet in 1951, when the first detachments of the Chinese People's Liberation Army invaded the high plateaus of the provinces in the east, Amdo and Kham. When Harrer died on January 10, 2006, the Dalai Lama mourned the loss of a personal friend and a defender of the rights of his people: "He came from a world that I did not know, and he taught me a lot about Europe especially. I thank him for having introduced Tibet and the Tibetans to the West, thanks to his book Seven Years in Tibet and to the lectures he gave throughout his life. We have lost a faithful Western friend, one who knew a free Tibet."[8]

I almost looked like
Moshe Dayan!

ONE OF THE ADVANTAGES of my life at the Potala was that there were many storerooms, which were a thousand times more fascinating to a little boy than the rooms housing priceless religious objects made of gold or silver; they were even more interesting than the *kudongs,* or burial monuments, sumptuous and studded with jewels, of my predecessors. I much preferred the armory, with its collection of swords, rifles, and coats of mail. But that was nothing compared to the incredible treasures in the rooms that contained certain objects that had belonged to my predecessors. Among them, I uncovered an old air rifle, with a complete set of targets and ammunition. I also discovered a telescope, not to mention the piles of illustrated books in English about the First World War. All this fascinated me and provided me with the inspiration for the models of ships, tanks, and planes that I invented. Later on, I asked that these books be translated into Tibetan. I also found two pairs of European shoes. Since my feet were much too small, I wore them with the toes stuffed with tissue. I was excited by the sound that the massive, hard heels made.

My favorite pastime was to take things apart and then try to put them back together. I ended up excelling in this activity, but in the beginning my efforts were not always crowned with success. I had notably discovered, among the belongings of the Thirteenth Dalai Lama, an old music box that had been presented by the czar of Russia. It didn't work, and I set about repairing it. I saw that the main spring was worn out and retracted. When I forced it with my screwdriver, the mechanism was suddenly and uncontrollably freed, and the little metal pieces flew out. I will never forget the diabolical symphony the pieces made as they flew in all directions all over the room. When I think back over the incident, I realize that I was lucky. I could have lost an eye, since my face was right next to the mechanism that I was fiddling with. I ran the risk of being mistaken for Moshe Dayan later on in life!

My Reincarnation Lineage

I am summoned to become the
Dalai Lama to serve others

I USED TO TALK CONSTANTLY with the gardeners, the servants, the sweepers. Most of them were simple people who treated me respectfully, since I was the Dalai Lama. There were also older people who were already expressing their hope, even at that early time, for a better future under my reign.

The oldest sweepers had known the Thirteenth Dalai Lama, since they had served under him. They told me a lot of anecdotes about his life. That helped me become aware of my future responsibilities. Later on, I thought that being the Dalai Lama was a difficult, complex position. It represented a real challenge, and the need to face it became increasingly imminent. As a Buddhist monk, I appreciate the value of my past lives. The virtue of good karma accumulated in my previous existences gives me, in my present life, many possibilities to help others and to serve the Buddha Dharma.[9] Thinking back on all this, I found and continue to find an additional motivation—a re-inforced desire to do everything I can for the welfare of others.

———————————

Progressively the little boy understood that he was called to assume high functions, a responsibility different from those of his brothers and other relatives. From the way others regarded him and acted toward him, he realized that he was the Dalai Lama even before he knew precisely what that implied. He saw that great things were expected of him, and he wanted to live up to the hopes people had in him. The task was a heavy one in a political context where the great neighboring countries, India and China, were agitated by unprecedented upheavals as imperialistic Britain and Russia quarreled over the Roof of the World. But the young sovereign saw a challenge in this situation, one he decided to meet by placing all his abilities at the service of the people.

As this part of the interview in which the Dalai Lama related his early years comes to an end, we are interrupted. A monk enters the interview room and murmurs a few words to the Dalai Lama, who immediately gets up, excusing himself, and leaves the room.

His private secretary explains that a great master has left his body. Mindroling Rinpoche died two days earlier. A delegation from his monastery has come to gather instructions about the rituals to perform and the arrangements to be made.

Twenty minutes later, the Dalai Lama is back. There is a veil of gravity in his eyes, but no sadness. In a confidential tone, he speaks about this lama who had been close to him and was just a little older. His death is a reminder of impermanence, in the Buddhist sense, which asserts the transitory quality of sentient beings and phenomena. Everything that is born from causes and conditions is perishable. Impermanence contradicts our feeling of the lasting quality of time and our human desire for immortality. It is unbearable for ordinary beings who have not trained their mind to conceive of the world's absence of reality. Denial of impermanence represents one of the main causes of suffering in our existences. Buddhist teachings invite us to contemplate and accept it.

The Tibetans will decide if they
want a Fifteenth Dalai Lama

Mindroling Rinpoche died two days ago. Since the time of the Fifth Dalai Lama, very special, strong links have existed between our lineages. He was seventy-eight years old, almost eighty. . . .

I don't know how many more years I will live, to eighty, ninety, a hundred. I don't know. . . . *(Laughs.)*

Today I'm over seventy, seventy-two exactly. So obviously . . . I am the Fourteenth Dalai Lama, and aside from the First,[10] I'm the one who has lived the longest. All the other Dalai Lamas stopped before seventy. So . . . *(laughs)* I'm very lucky! *(Laughs.)*

At the same time, as a Buddhist practitioner, I meditate constantly on impermanence. Now, in my own case, impermanence is becoming a reality. A reality that's closer and closer. . . .

In 1969 I had already anticipated that and made arrangements, making it clear that it would depend entirely on the Tibetan people to decide if the institution of the Dalai Lama should continue or not. At that time, some Tibetans expressed their concerns about what would happen after me and in the period following my death. I expressed the opinion that if a majority of Tibetans wanted to preserve the institution of the Dalai Lamas, they should consider several options.

Things are constantly changing. We must act according to a new reality where Tibet is concerned and take into consideration, today, not only the Tibetans but also the Mongolians, who have traditionally been closely connected with the institution of the Dalai Lamas. If these peoples want to keep the Dalai Lamas, they should adhere to the custom of looking for my new incarnation according to ritual. Given that the obvious aim of a reincarnation is to continue the task that hasn't been finished by his predecessor, then logically, if my death occurs while I am outside of Tibet, my reincarnation will manifest abroad in order to complete what I have left unfinished.

But there are also other possibilities. Many years ago I explained that, according to Tibetan tradition, the process of succession can be determined in a different way.

My Dalailamaship

I T WAS MY WISH that temporal authority be handed over to a prime minister, the Kalon Tripa, and he was elected for the first time in 2001. So now I'm part-time, and I'm sometimes asked if I plan on retiring. Is that possible? Can my Dalailamaship retire?

No, I cannot become a retiree (*laughs*). Unless a majority no longer regards me as the Dalai Lama—then I'll be able to go into retirement! (*laughs*).

I'm joking!

Since 2001, we have had a leader of the executive branch elected by vote every five years. That is how I could go into semi-retirement in politics. In Tibet, in 1952, I initiated changes that were the preliminaries for democratization. But we weren't able to set in motion our modernization program, since so many upheavals happened.

Then, when we arrived in India as refugees, we were all favorable to democracy. Since 2001, the main decisions have been made by people who were elected, and not by me. In fact, I act as an experienced adviser. In 2006, Samdhong Rinpoche was reelected, and the rule is that one can only serve for two terms.[11] So in four years a new person will be chosen by election.

I don't think it is important to preserve the institution of the Dalai Lama. We should make a clear distinction between safeguarding Tibetan culture and Tibetan Buddhism, on the one hand, and preserving the office of the Dalai Lama, on the other. This institution, like others, appears at a given moment in time and then disappears; Tibetan Buddhism and its cultural heritage, however, will remain as long as the Tibetan people.

That is why in 1992 I declared that, when the time has come for us to go back to our homeland, to Tibet—that is, when we have won a real autonomy—then I will hand over all my legitimate authority as Dalai Lama to the Tibetan government.[12]

Why shouldn't a very beautiful
woman be my next incarnation?

I N THE PAST, certain reincarnations were recognized before the death of their predecessors, who chose qualified successors. In my generation, this sort of occurrence may come about, depending on the particular circumstances at a given time.

Westerners are fascinated by the idea that the next incarnation of the Dalai Lama could be a woman. Theoretically, yes, that is possible. The profound reason for reincarnation is to carry out the task that wasn't completed in the previous life. Logically, if my death occurs during exile, my reincarnation will come from abroad in order to finish what I began.

The very goal of reincarnation is to serve the Buddha Dharma. In Buddhist teaching, men and women have the same basic rights. But in reality, two thousand five hundred years ago Indian tradition posited the preeminence of monks. Although higher ordinations are theoretically accessible to nuns in the Buddhist community, in Tibet, Sri Lanka, and Thailand nuns were prevented from receiving the highest ordinations. In Tibet this type of ordination was conferred on monks by Shantarakshita, while nuns were excluded.[13] Fortunately, in China the tradition of higher ordination for nuns was maintained to this day. There are discussions today about reintroducing higher ordination for women.

Even so, in Tibetan tradition there are lineages of female high reincarnations, like Dorje Phagmo, a lineage that is over six hundred years old. I don't know if these reincarnate women are all nuns or not, but in most cases I think they have taken vows. Consequently, according to circumstances, if a Dalai Lama in a female form can help beings better serve the Buddha Dharma, why deprive ourselves of that?

Beauty is one of the eight qualities of a precious human body on the physical level. It is obvious that if a female Dalai Lama is ugly to look at, she will attract fewer people. The aim of a female reincarnation is to transmit the Buddhist teachings to the public in a convincing way. That would not be to spend twenty-four hours a day meditating and chanting prayers. From this point of view, the question of appearance has its importance. Consequently, I sometimes tell people, half-joking, that if I reincarnate as a woman, naturally I will be a very beautiful woman physically.

I don't know if I will appoint the next Dalai Lama during my lifetime. It is a possibility I am contemplating. Let's have people give their advice, then we'll see. In the past, about a decade ago, this point was debated among the main Tibetan lineage holders. In the months to come, we will probably have a meeting on this subject, as well as on the ordination of women.

———————

The Tibetan clergy includes a majority of male lamas, and rebirth as a male is traditionally considered better, even though Tibetan Buddhists glorify the feminine as a symbol of wisdom and venerate Tara the Liberator, whose vow to attain Enlightenment as a woman was fulfilled.

There are lineages of female lamas, but it is rare for reincarnate lamas not to be the same sex as their previous incarnations. So the Dalai Lama's declarations about his successor are unusual. It is true that His Holiness the Fourteenth Dalai Lama has continually surprised people with his bold reforms; in adapting the age-old customs of Tibet to the modern world, he has been concerned with preserving the spirit of those customs rather than their outer form. It would seem that he is preparing to break new ground on the sensitive point of his succession, which calls into question the tulku system,[14] cornerstone of Tibetan Buddhism.

We are without beginning or end

THE CONCEPT of a line of incarnation for the Dalai Lamas presumes the continuity between two living beings: the predecessor and his reincarnation.

Buddhism accepts the existence of the continuity of a being. The Buddhist theory of "selflessness" means that there is no independent self apart from the body, because "self" or the person is designated by the combination of body and mind. There is a self, but there is no independent absolute self. With respect to continuation, not only does Buddhism accept the continuity of the being, but it also upholds the notion of a "beginningless" self, that is, a self with no beginning and no end until Buddhahood is achieved.

There are different kinds of reincarnations. An eminent Buddha, or *bodhisattva,* can manifest several times simultaneously; lower bodhisattvas reincarnate only in one person—that is, once at a time. But anyone, irrespective of whether they are a bodhisattva or an ordinary person, is reborn from "beginninglessness" and will be born endlessly. Continuity is always there and will always be there, owing to karma. Now, at one stage, if you develop a certain spiritual realization, then the birth through karma will cease. Then, with will power, you can choose your rebirth. This type of rebirth we call reincarnation.[15]

I could reincarnate in the
form of an insect

RECOGNITION OF REINCARNATE LAMAS, or tulkus, is more logical than it might seem at first. Given the Buddhist belief that the principle of reincarnation is an established fact and that the only point of a reincarnation is to allow someone to continue his efforts to liberate all sentient beings from suffering, we can acknowledge that it is possible to identify children who are the rebirths of certain people. That allows us to train them and establish them in the world so that they can continue their task as soon as possible. Of course mistakes can happen in the process of recognition, but the effectiveness of the system is attested by the lives of a great majority of tulkus. (Several hundred have been recognized today, whereas in Tibet, before the Chinese invasion, there were probably thousands.)

The process of identification is less mysterious than you might think. First of all, one proceeds by elimination. Let's take the example of a search for a certain monk. First you have to establish the time and place of his death. If you think, according to your experience, that the new incarnation will in principle be conceived in the next year, you set up a calendar. So if Lama X died in Year Y, his next incarnation will probably be born eighteen months to two years later. In Year Y plus five, the child will probably be around three or four years old. So already you have narrowed the field of investigation down.

Then you define the most probable place of birth. Usually that's quite easy. First you ask yourself if it will be in Tibet or elsewhere. If it is abroad, there are a limited number of places—in Tibetan communities in India, Nepal, or Switzerland, for instance. Then you decide in what city you are most likely to find the child. This probability is deduced with reference to the life of the previous incarnation.

The next step is to gather together a search party. This does not necessarily mean that a group of people will be dispatched, as if for a treasure hunt. Generally, it is enough to investigate among a community to find out if a three- or four-year-old child is a likely candidate. Often you have useful clues, like unusual phenomena that occurred at birth. Or else a child might demonstrate unusual qualities.

Sometimes two or three possibilities—or more—present themselves at this stage. Or a search party might prove to be unnecessary, since the previous incarnation left detailed information about the name of his successor and the names of his parents. But that is rather rare. In other cases, disciples of the monk can have lucid dreams or visions indicating where the reincarnation can be found. The rules are not rigid or fixed.

The purpose of a reincarnation is to facilitate the continuation of a being's work, which can have important consequences, depending on the person who is being sought. For example, in my case, even if my efforts in general are devoted to the service of all beings, I direct them more particularly to my Tibetan compatriots. So if I die before Tibet has found its freedom again, logically I will be reborn outside of Tibet. If at that moment my people no longer need a Dalai Lama, then it will not be necessary to search for me. So I could be reborn as an insect, or an animal, or some other form of existence that is useful to the greatest number of sentient beings.

To ensure its control over Tibetan society, the Chinese Communist Party assumed the right to control reincarnation lineages. So that they are not seques-

tered by Beijing authorities, child lamas are placed under careful protection by their families. In the greatest secrecy, smugglers take them to Nepal or India. There they join monasteries that provide a religious education suitable for their future responsibilities.

In May 1995, the Dalai Lama confirmed Gendhun Chökyi Nyima, a six-year-old boy, as the reincarnation of the Tenth Panchen Lama, the second-highest dignitary in Tibetan Buddhism. Two days later the Chinese Council of Religious Affairs declared this choice "illegal and invalid." The same day the religious dignitary in charge of the search for the child lama, Chadral Rinpoche, was arrested and imprisoned for collusion with "the Dalai Lama clique." A few weeks later the Eleventh Panchen Lama and his parents disappeared. Ever since July 1995, he has been kept in a supervised residence in a place held secret, thus becoming the youngest political prisoner in the world. Legislating like King Ubu in religious affairs, the Chinese Communist Party chose another child and enthroned him in a puppet ceremony. Despite the repeated protests of the international community, we are still without news of Gendhun Chökyi Nyima, the recognized Eleventh Panchen Lama according to authentic ritual.

Recently, the Chinese authorities made known their desire to exercise increased control over lineages. Thus, in August 2007 the official Chinese news agency announced a new rule about the recognition of "living buddhas," an expression the Chinese use to designate reincarnate masters. Henceforth, "all requests for recognition of a reincarnation of a 'living buddha' must be approved by the Bureau of Religious Affairs," under penalty of law.

The Dalai Lama has commented on these measures with humor: "This bizarre decision proves that its authors, who somehow pride themselves in delivering 'reincarnation permits,' understand nothing about either reincarnation or Buddhism. They think all that's necessary is a decree or a rule to extend their control over people's minds. It doesn't work like that. If *they were even a tiny bit attentive to the reality that's all around them, they would realize this."*[16]

This regulatory control over lineages occurs in a context where the age of the Fourteenth Dalai Lama inevitably poses the question of his succession. Beijing has decided to regulate succession, scorning the moral and spiritual right of the Tibetans. According to Samdhong Rinpoche, prime minister of the Tibetan government in exile, "It is not the Dalai Lama who took the initiative to talk about his succession, but the People's Republic of China. The Chinese are very anxious about his reincarnation, which they want to choose themselves. So they hope that the present Fourteenth holder of the title won't live much longer, and they spread rumors saying the Dalai Lama has terminal cancer, so they can try to guess the nomination of his successor. It is clear that they're doing everything they can to impose a new Dalai Lama under their control. It is crucial for the Tibetan people to define the designation procedure for the Fifteenth Dalai Lama.

"His Holiness is the only one, since the First Dalai Lama, to have lived so long, and he has to consider his succession, since his job isn't over yet. The problem of a regency comes up. It is too complex to wait for a child Dalai Lama to grow up until he's an adult. His Holiness had to take on his responsibilities when he was very young, and that was difficult. His successor will have to be of an age to take on his functions when the time comes. That is why the Dalai Lama is thinking about appointing a madé tulku during his lifetime, literally a 'reincarnation before death,' following a tradition by which the master, before dying, transfers the essence of his spiritual realization to his successor."

In the speech he gave when he presented the Nobel Peace Prize to the Dalai Lama, Egil Aarvik observed: "The process of recognizing a reincarnation implies entering what is, for a Westerner, terra incognita, where beliefs, thought and action exist in a dimension of existence of which we are ignorant, or that perhaps we have simply forgotten."[17]

Even if the Dalai Lama readily states that he is "no one special," his life is not ordinary, in the sense that it does not begin with his birth and will not end with his death. The holder of the lineage of awakened Compassion, he radiates from a universal dimension. How do profound states of awareness contribute to this, revealed by meditation and Buddhist practice? That is what his statements as a monk in the following chapter will reveal. They shed light on the formidable humanity of a human being who "makes us feel good about being human. About being alive at a time when someone like him is around." [18]

PART TWO

As a
Buddhist Monk

3

Transforming
Oneself

My Ideal: The Bodhisattva

My identity as a monk

I OFTEN INTRODUCE MYSELF AS a simple Buddhist monk because my personality and my identity have been built around my commitment as a monk. Although I sometimes feel a very strong karmic link with the Dalai Lamas who came before me, I consider myself a monk first of all. I am a monk before I am the Dalai Lama!

This is such a clear certainty, and it's so deeply rooted in my mind, that I even remember it when I'm dreaming. Even during the worst part of a nightmare, I don't forget that I am a monk. But I've never dreamed I was the Dalai Lama.

By my lights, these reactions at a level beyond intellectual control prove that at the bottom of my heart there is the indelible imprint of my state as a monk. I feel very intensely the fact that I am a simple Buddhist monk.

My monk's vows

IN TIBETAN MONASTICISM, there are 253 rules for monks and 364 for nuns. By observing them as scrupulously as possible, I free myself from useless distractions and everyday concerns. Some of these rules have a lot to do with etiquette—stipulating, for instance, how far a monk should walk behind the abbot of his monastery. Others have to do with conduct.

The four root vows correspond to four simple prohibitions: a monk must not kill, steal, or lie about his spiritual realizations, and he must also observe strict chastity. If he breaks one of these four vows, he is no longer a monk.

I am sometimes asked if it's really desirable to maintain the vow of chastity and if such a vow can be kept. It should be said that this practice does not amount to suppressing sexual desire. On the contrary, it is necessary to accept fully the existence of such desire and to transcend it through the exercise of reason. When you manage to do this, there results a mastery of the mind that is very beneficial. Sexual desire is blind, and that poses a problem. When you say to yourself, *I want to have sex with that person,* you are expressing a desire that the intelligence does not direct. On the other hand, when you think, *I want to eradicate poverty from the world,* that is an intellectually controllable desire. What's more, sexual gratification represents only an ephemeral satisfaction. As the great Indian sage Nagarjuna said: "When you have an itch, you scratch yourself. But not having an itch at all is better than scratching yourself for a long time."

The daily meditations of
a Buddhist monk

I SPEND AT LEAST five and a half hours a day praying, meditating, or studying. I also pray during all the idle moments throughout the day, during meals or traveling. As a Buddhist, I don't see any difference between religious practice and daily life. Religious practice is a 24/7 occupation. There are also prayers prescribed for every activity, from waking up to bathing, eating, and even sleeping. For tantric practitioners, exercises performed during deep sleep and dreaming are some of the most important, since they prepare us for dying.

My main meditation concerns emptiness and consists in concentrating on interdependence on the subtlest level. Part of this practice involves "deity yoga," in which I use different mandalas, visualizing myself as a series of deities. (I don't mean by this beings that exist externally or independently.) As I do this, I focus my mind on a level where it is no longer solicited by the data that sensory awareness transmits. It is not a trance, since I remain fully lucid, but rather an exercise in *pure awareness*.

It is hard to realize what I mean by this, as hard as it is for a scientist to explain through words what he means by *space-time*. Neither language nor everyday experience can translate the experience of pure awareness, mastery of which is acquired over many years.

One important aspect of my daily practice concerns the idea of death. In my opinion, there are only two things to do in life on the subject of death. Either you choose to ignore it—in which case you might be lucky enough to chase the idea away for a while—or you confront this prospect, you try to analyze it, and by doing so you try to diminish certain inevitable sufferings it causes. Neither method can fully achieve its goal.

As a Buddhist, I accept death as a normal process of life. I accept it as a reality that will occur for as long as I remain in samsara. Knowing that I cannot escape it, I don't see the point of worrying about it. I think that dying is a little like leaving behind used old clothing. It is not an end in itself.

As a Buddhist, I also believe that the experience of death is essential. It is at that moment that the most profound and beneficial experiences can manifest. For this reason, there are many great spiritual masters who take leave of earthly existence during meditation. When that occurs, their bodies don't decompose until long after clinical death.

Living as a bodhisattva

As FOR MY PERSONAL RELIGIOUS PRACTICE, I try to live my life by following what I call the "bodhisattva ideal." In Buddhist conception, a bodhisattva is a being who is engaged on the path toward Buddhahood and is completely devoted to helping sentient beings liberate themselves from suffering. The word *bodhisattva* is easier to understand if the two terms that make it up, *bodhi* and *sattva*, are translated separately. *Bodhi* stands for the wisdom that understands the ultimate nature of reality, and *sattva* is a person motivated by universal compassion. So the bodhisattva ideal amounts to an aspiration to practice infinite compassion with infinite wisdom.

Spiritual practice in order to become better human beings

Do NOT EXPECT extraordinary things of me, like omnipotent blessings that could transform your life miraculously and instantaneously. You would be wrong to entertain such thoughts—they have nothing to do with reality. I am a simple Buddhist monk who has been practicing since the age of ten and who tries to live according to the Buddha's teachings.

As a simple monk, I am an interpreter of that sublime master before whom I prostrate with humility. When the Buddha was alive, he looked like an ordinary monk; he traveled on foot, holding his beggar's bowl. After him, many great practitioners have had that same outer appearance, which might seem contemptible if one didn't look beyond appearances.

We share in common with the Buddha the same potential for goodness and serenity. But we don't always know this, and sometimes we manage to destroy both the happiness of others and our own inner peace. We all want to avoid suffering and be happy. We have an intimate experiential knowledge of both happiness and suffering that is common to all sentient beings.

I am sharing with you my experience of life, based on Buddhist teaching and practice, without any desire to propagate Buddhism or make new followers. The great spiritual traditions, which are all very much alive on the five continents, reflect the various dispositions of the peoples of the world. They define the foundations and ethical principles that will allow us to become better by developing human qualities like love, patience, and tolerance and by fighting our excessive desires.

It is preferable to keep to our original spiritual traditions. That is a much surer path. I am always a little doubtful when I teach Buddhism in a country like France, which is mostly Christian and Catholic, for I am convinced that it is always more satisfying to deepen and preserve the religion of one's ancestors. It is not necessary to become Buddhist when you are a Westerner.

If you examine the great religions of the world, you can discern philosophical and metaphysical views, on the one hand, and daily spiritual practice, on the other. Although the philosophical views differ and sometimes contradict each other, in spiritual practice all religions are connected. They all recommend inner transformation of our stream of consciousness, which will make us better, more devout people.

It is good not to create any hierarchy among spiritual traditions but rather to understand that their teachings are adapted to the various dispositions of beings. What's more, within Buddhism itself you can find many teachings of the Buddha, who taught a doctrine that is described as having "84,000 doors." It is up to us to recognize the necessity of different philosophical views and to acknowledge that every spiritual tradition is good, since each one helps millions of people to progress and to suffer less by becoming better. For each person, there is one single way and one single truth to acquire, but one must still accept the truth of other traditions. Even if another tradition goes against our own convictions, it has its own reason for being, in the support it provides for others. So we should have our own convictions, on the one hand, but on the other hand, we should keep our minds open and tolerant toward those who don't share them.

Temples of Kindness in Our Hearts

Toward brotherly exchanges between religions

A S WE APPROACH the twenty-first century, religious traditions are as relevant as ever. Yet, as in the past, conflicts and crises arise in the name of different religious traditions. This is very, very unfortunate. We must make every effort to overcome this situation. In my own experience, I have found that the most effective method to overcome these conflicts is close contact and an exchange among those of various beliefs, not only on an intellectual level but in deeper spiritual experiences. This is a powerful method to develop mutual understanding and respect. Through this exchange, a strong foundation of genuine harmony can be established.

In addition to encounters among scholars and experienced practitioners, it is also important, particularly in the eyes of the public, that leaders of the various religious traditions occasionally come together to meet and pray, as in the important meeting at Assisi in 1986. This is a simple yet effective way to promote tolerance and understanding.

Politicians need religion more than hermits

I HAVE HAD MANY FASCINATING CONVERSATIONS with the Archbishop of Canterbury, Dr. Robert Runcie (whose admirable envoy, Terry Waite, I always keep in my prayers). We share the viewpoint that religion and politics can come together effectively, and we both agree that, obviously, the duty of religion is to serve humanity. Religion should not ignore reality. It is not enough for members of a religious order to devote themselves to prayer. They are morally obligated to contribute as much as possible to solving the world's problems.

I remember an Indian politician who invited me to discuss this point with him. He said to me, with sincere humility, "Oh, but we're politicians, not monks!" To which I replied: "Politicians need religion even more than a hermit in retreat. If the hermit acts inspired by bad motivation, he'll harm only himself. But if a politician, who can directly influence an entire society, acts with bad motivation, a large number of people will experience the negative consequences."

I don't see any contradiction between politics and religion. For in fact, what is religion? Where I am concerned, I regard every action carried out with good motivation as religious. On the other hand, people who have gathered in a temple or a church without good motivation are not behaving religiously when they pray together.

My pilgrimages, from Lourdes to Jerusalem

I AM FIRMLY CONVINCED that we can further understanding and harmony among religions and thus promote world peace. To accomplish this, I encourage interfaith exchanges, especially pilgrimages. That is why I visited Lourdes, in southern France, not as a tourist but as a pilgrim. I drank the holy water, I stopped in front of the statue of Mary, and I realized that in this place millions of people receive a blessing or a feeling of calm. As I was looking at Mary, I felt rising up within me a sincere admiration and an authentic respect for Christianity, which benefits such a large number of people. The Christian religion does, of course, have a different philosophy from my own, but the aid and concrete benefits it brings are undeniable.

It was in the same spirit that in 1993 I went to Jerusalem, the holy site of so many great religions in the world. I meditated at the Wailing Wall with Jewish friends, and then, in Christian places of worship, I prayed with Christian friends. Then I visited the holy site of our Muslim friends, and I prayed there with them.

I have also gone to different Hindu, Jain, and Sikh temples, to Zoroastrian holy places in India, and elsewhere. I have prayed or shared in silent meditation with the followers of these traditions.

More recently, I joined Christian and Buddhist leaders for a pilgrimage to Bodhgaya in India. Every morning we sat under the Bodhi Tree for a communal meditation session. Since the time of the Buddha over 2,500 years ago and the time of Jesus Christ 2,000 years ago, I think that was the first time such an encounter occurred.

There is a place that I've wanted to visit for a long time, but this wish has not yet been fulfilled. It is the Wu Tai Shan, the mountain of Five Terraces, venerated in China and dedicated to Manjushri, the bodhisattva of Wisdom. My predecessor, the Thirteenth Dalai Lama, went there to pay homage, and during my first trip to China in 1954 I wished to follow in his footsteps. At that time the Chinese authorities refused my request, under the pretext that the roads were unfit for travel.

A life of contemplation
on love

ON A VISIT TO THE GREAT MONASTERY at Montserrat in Spain, I met a Benedictine monk there. He came especially to see me—and his English was much poorer than mine, so I felt more courage to speak to him. After lunch we spent some time alone, face to face, and I was informed that this monk had spent a few years in the mountains just behind the monastery. I asked him what kind of contemplation he had practiced during those years of solitude. His answer was simple: "Love, love, love." How wonderful! I suppose that sometimes he also slept. But during all those years he meditated simply on love. And he was not meditating on just the word. When I looked into his eyes, I saw evidence of profound spirituality and love—as I had during my meetings with Thomas Merton.

Temples *inside*

I BELIEVE THE PURPOSE of all the major religious traditions is not to construct big temples on the outside, but to create temples of goodness and compassion *inside,* in our hearts.

Some people believe that the most reasonable way to attain harmony and solve problems relating to religious intolerance is to establish one universal religion for everyone. However, I have always felt that we should have different religious traditions because human beings possess so many different mental dispositions: one religion simply cannot satisfy the needs of such a variety of people. If we try to unify the faiths of the world into one religion, we will also lose many of the qualities and richnesses of each particular tradition. Therefore, I feel it is better, in spite of the many quarrels in the name of religion, to maintain a variety of religious traditions. Unfortunately, while a diversity of religious traditions is more suited to serve the needs of the diverse mental dispositions among humanity, this diversity naturally possesses the potential for conflict and disagreement as well. Consequently, people of every religious tradition must make an extra effort to transcend intolerance and misunderstanding and seek harmony.[1]

Transforming Our Minds

Analysis of the mind as a preliminary to spiritual practice

To FREE OURSELVES FROM SUFFERING, we must understand what happens before suffering. For nothing appears without causes or conditions. It's up to us to recognize the causes that increase suffering or diminish it. That is part of the analysis of the mind, an indispensable preliminary to spiritual practice.

The mind is subject to circumstantial pressures; it fluctuates with them and reacts to the impact of sensations. Material progress and a higher standard of living improve comfort and health but do not lead to a transformation of the mind, the only thing capable of providing lasting peace. Profound happiness, unlike fleeting pleasures, is spiritual by nature. It depends on the happiness of others, and it is based on love and tenderness. We would be wrong to think that being happy consists of grasping the best at others' expense. The lack of altruism, which causes family discord and disturbance, causes solitude. We should take care not to be excessively concerned with the external world, realizing that grasping and owning material goods reinforce self-centeredness.

The key to happiness lies in strength of mind, inner serenity, and a quality like steadfastness. We can approach this by developing tenderness and love, which correspond to the profound nature of every human being. The mother-child relationship is probably the best example of the non-ordinary love of loving someone else more than yourself. The first word each of us has uttered is "mama," and in just about every language this word contains the syllable *ma*. Another monosyllabic word in most languages in the world, with the exception of Japanese, designates the self: "me" (or "mine") indicates the extreme attachment we have for our own person. It is an attachment we must fight in order to spread altruistic qualities.

Of course, one can cultivate human qualities without having a religion. But as a general rule, religion allows us to increase these qualities more effectively.

Impermanence and interdependence, or seeing the world as it is

BUDDHISM OFFERS A METHOD that will improve us while reflecting the true nature of things, without letting us be fooled by appearances. Phenomena, which manifest to our faculties of perception, have no ultimate reality. Let us take the example of a mountain. It seems to be the same today as it was yesterday. Formed thousands of years ago, it represents a continuity in the world of phenomena. Although we can note a relative stability in its appearance on a coarse level, we must still acknowledge that each of its particles, on a very subtle level, is changing from one instant to the next. Change, on the infinitesimal level, is accompanied in our mind by an appearance of continuity. Yet the continuity thus perceived is illusory. For nothing remains the same, and no two consecutive instants are alike.

After the example of the mountain, let's take that of the flower, whose fragility and ephemeral nature are obvious. The flower that is blooming today was first a seed, then a bud. These changes of state illustrate the subtle impermanence of every instant, which is the true nature of the flower: it is doomed to rapid destruction. Whether it is a question of a mountain or a flower, we must get used to understanding that the instant a phenomenon appears it carries within it the cause of its own end.

The impermanence of phenomena depends on external causes and conditions. To say that all things are interdependent means that they have no inherent existence. The very potential for transformation at work in phenomena is a sign of the fundamental reciprocity of life.

Can we determine that a "flower" entity as such exists in itself? The answer is no. The flower is only a collection of characteristics—form, color, smell—but no "flower" exists independent of its appearances.

Our perception of time also rests on a mistaken apprehension of reality. What in fact is the past? The past is not a reality; it's just a concept. The future corresponds to projections, anticipations that do not have any reality either. The past has already occurred; the future does not yet exist. These notions affect us as realities, although they have no substance. The present is the truth that we are experiencing here and now, but it is an elusive reality that does not last. We find ourselves in a paradoxical situation in which the present constitutes a border, a limit between a past and a future without any concrete reality. The present is that elusive moment between what no longer exists and what has not yet happened.

These notions that we take as "reality" are pure intellectual fabrications that do not involve an independent reality, existent in itself. According to the Buddha, perceived phenomena exist only from the standpoint of their designation—that is, the names and concepts we attach to them. The functioning of phenomena does not reveal a palpable entity that is uniquely theirs. You could compare phenomena to a mirage: the closer you get to it, the farther away it gets, until it disappears. Similarly faced with the mind that analyzes them, phenomena vanish.

So we should distinguish two truths: a relative truth, which concerns the appearance of phenomena, their emergence, their manifestation, and their cessation; and an ultimate truth, which recognizes the absence of inherent reality in phenomena. By saying that phenomena are empty of intrinsic existence, we are declaring not their nonexistence but their interdependence, their absence of concrete reality. And the emptiness of phenomena, far from being a mental construct or a concept, corresponds to the reality itself of the phenomenal world.

The Buddha does not deny that things appear, but posits the union of appearance and emptiness. Thus, the flower exists: its forms and characteristics are inscribed in our mind. But its nature is devoid of any intrinsic existence.

Transforming our mind
on the Buddha's path

MORE THAN JUST A PHILOSOPHICAL VIEW of the world, Buddhism represents a path of transforming the mind, with the aim of freeing ourselves from suffering and its causes. Transforming the mind involves first learning to know it, then identifying how it functions so as to eliminate the three main mental poisons, which are ignorance, desire, and hatred. So it is beneficial to analyze the stream of our consciousness and its variations. Understanding the ultimate nature of consciousness, without beginning or end, whose continuum is distinct from the physical support of the coarse body, is the foundation that allows us to realize the primordial purity of the mind.

Buddhist analysis of reality concurs with the conclusions of quantum physics, according to which particles of matter are real while still being devoid of ultimate solidity. Similarly, in Buddhism the phenomena that exist in interdependence are empty of intrinsic, autonomous existence. Interdependence is a universal concept. Nothing can occur without causes or conditions. Causality, or *karma*, is the law that governs the world of phenomena. A dynamic flux of changing appearances occurs, responding to causes and effects. But that does not mean that we should think there is an original, unchanging, permanent cause, like an organizing principle. In a world that is constantly changing, mutations are due to qualities that are inherent in phenomena.

Once we have established the conditions for the appearance of the elements of the phenomenal world, we can proceed to an analysis of the mechanisms that create the contrasting states of happiness and suffering in our mind.

Every living being has a basic aspiration to attain happiness and avoid suffering. How are the happiness and suffering we experience linked to the world outside us? Faced with the external world, we have reactions that are expressed in the form of sensations possessing various characteristics. We then evaluate these sensations and connect the experience of them to ourselves as experiencers.

Happiness and suffering do not necessarily have an immediate sensory cause. According to science, electrochemical processes inside the brain are the source of all our mental experiences. But physiological functioning does not account for experiences of subtle awareness. Buddhism does not restrict consciousness to the brain. Meditation and contemplation induce subtle, profound states of mind that themselves have the power to modify physiological processes. Indeed, consciousness is linked to our physical body, but it is not limited to it. Consciousness represents a faculty of clarity and luminosity that allows us to perceive and know phenomena by direct apprehension.

Consciousness produces experiences such as dreams, where we experience happiness and suffering, but these sensations have no substantial object as their basis. We distinguish between waking consciousness, dream consciousness, and the consciousness of profound sleep, which do not depend exclusively on the sense organs. When we are distracted, the eye sees but the consciousness does not register the image. Pure consciousness is the pure faculty of cognition in its essential, naked state.

Consciousness is, of course, associated with the body, but it is qualitatively different from the coarse physical body, since the causes and conditions that maintain it have their autonomy. Consciousness is not interrupted, even when we faint, and it persists in the states of dream and sleep, where the link with the support of the body is altered. We can go so far as to say that the physical support is not necessary for experiences where the consciousness detaches itself from the body and changes without being connected to it. If consciousness were solely substantial and material, then just as there is a biological continuity between parents and children, so there would be a similarity of experience between them on the conscious level. Obviously, this is not the case.

If we had to conceive of a beginning to the phenomenon of consciousness, it would be in the form of a first cause, and perhaps we could argue that it arose from transformations in the inanimate world. That is not satisfactory on the logical level, so it is preferable to envisage a continuity of consciousness. Each instant of consciousness stems from a previous instant of consciousness. What we call a person is a concept attached to a stream of consciousness. This stream, just like the person, is without beginning or end. It is a question of an ephemeral continuum that depends on changing causes and conditions.

Actualizing our potential

IGNORANCE MAY BE DEFINED AS a mistaken mode of perception that posits belief in the autonomous solidity of the self and of phenomena. Such a mode of perception corresponds to the natural functioning of the mind, reinforced by long-standing habit. Analysis allows us to discover that things have neither reality nor solidity. The perception resulting from the ultimate analysis of things should be cultivated and used as antidote. That is how we will fight the deep-rooted propensity that leads us to believe in the reality of the self and the world.

Fighting ignorance is also fighting suffering. Ignorance is the source of the mental poisons and obscurations. By developing altruism, love, tenderness, and compassion, we reduce hatred, desire, and pride. But a subtle form of mental obscuration remains that can be overcome by one antidote alone, which is the realization of a complete absence of identity of phenomena and identity of the self. As long as grasping and fixating on the self and on phenomena persist, the cause of suffering cannot be eliminated. To eradicate suffering, we must cultivate stable qualities in the mental continuum that will become second nature. These qualities are born from the correct perception of reality. Wisdom and lasting serenity result from this, for they are linked to consciousness itself.

The natural luminosity of awareness is the antidote to the mental poisons, which are the effects of mental constructions based on the ephemeral adventitious veils that obscure natural awareness and cause suffering. How, then, can we bring about the absence of suffering?

Wisdom is the surest antidote that can dissipate our fundamental ignorance. Dharma—that is, the teaching of the Buddha—brings knowledge that is useful to eliminate disturbing emotions and the subtlest forms of ignorance. Dharma leads us beyond suffering to nirvana. The Buddha is called the Bhagavan—in Tibetan, "One who has destroyed the four Maras,"[2] which are death, distraction, pride, and the emotional obscurations. The Dharma allows us to conquer the mental factors that act as obstacles to Enlightenment, and it gives us access to nirvana, a state that is beyond the emotional obscurations.

Aryadeva tells us: "In the beginning, we must abandon all negative actions; in the middle, all attachment to ego; and in the end, all extremes, opinions or concepts."[3] To obtain such a realization, we must unite wisdom with inner accomplishment. Theoretical knowledge and intellectual conviction are not enough. We ourselves must reflect, in life circumstances that are a teaching, in order to validate the doctrine by means of personal experience and authentic familiarization. Meditation is the gradual process that acclimates us to a new vision.

Study produces certainty only if, through steady practice, we transform our mind and master the inner space of awareness. The case is often cited of a scholar who devoted himself only to study, without cultivating any inner accomplishment, and was reborn as a ghost with the head of a donkey.

To win the conditions that will allow us to understand the ultimate nature of things—and the immense compassion resulting from that realization—we first use the mind for discursive thinking, then gradually let the continuum of natural luminosity appear on the surface of the mind. There are many methods: *Anuyoga,* for instance, relies on the breath, the channels, and the essences[4] to let primordial wisdom arise; the *Kalachakra* system actualizes the ultimate nature of the mind by joining bliss and emptiness; and *Atiyoga* directly apprehends enlightened presence. The point of all these different methods is to dissolve the aggregates into light. In our tradition, that is the rainbow body that the great practitioners manifest when they die.

Thus, in eastern Tibet, they say that before he died one monk asked that no one touch his corpse for a week and that the door to his room remain closed. After seven days, when they went into the room, his body had completely dissolved. They found only his monastic robes; even his nails and hair had disappeared. This monk was a hermit who lived very simply, without externalizing any signs of realization during his life devoted to contemplation. He had managed, through his practice, to actualize the primordial purity of the mind.

We are not all called to such an accomplishment. It is better, for our daily practice, to stay at home, keeping our professional and family life while still learning to become better from day to day and adhering to a positive mode of life that will contribute to the good of society, according to the principles of the Dharma. We should choose professions in the areas of education, health, or social services. We should avoid renouncing everything for a solitary retreat. The aim is not to devote ourselves solely to spiritual practice, to lead a life lost in the glaciers. We should progress by degrees, steadily, taking care not to have extreme views, in a spirit of steadfastness and perseverance.

Practice is essential, for it renews the inner life. Discipline, contemplation, and wisdom are the three trainings that will allow an authentic transmutation. "If we haven't transformed ourselves, how will we help others transform themselves?" asks the Tibetan saint Tsongkhapa.[5]

Progressively we get accustomed to transforming our perceptions, our ways of thinking, and our behavior. It is a question of bringing about a complete reversal of mental habits by reducing emotions in a gradual process of study, reflection, and meditation—in other words, familiarization. That is how we refine the mind and purify it through a training that actualizes its potential. We learn to master the stream of our consciousness, to control the emotional obscurations, without letting ourselves be dominated by them. That is the path toward realization of the absolute nature. Our practice integrates all the aspects and all the various levels of the Buddha's teaching.

Faced with the emotional obscurations, we must learn to be constantly vigilant. When one of them presents itself to our mind, we should react as if a thief has gotten into our house, and we should be quick to chase it away. For it is our spiritual realizations that are about to be stolen from us. If the mental poisons can finally be transformed into wisdom, it is because their ultimate nature is endowed with primordial, naturally luminous purity.

Training our emotional life

THE SELF IS THE ROOT of the mental poisons. Our mind fabricates, projects, and attaches concepts to people and things. Egocentric fixation reinforces the qualities or defects that we attribute to others. From this results a solidification of the separation between me and not-me, mine and not-mine. Things we perceive as separate are actually connected, but our "I" separates them. So long as we are in ignorance and have not experienced the absence of reality of the self, our mind believes in its solidity. Realizing the absence of inherent existence of the self is an effective antidote to egocentric fixation, and it is the point of the teachings on the Buddha's path.

Under the effect of attraction and desire, the mind mixes with and attaches itself to the object of its craving. Desire for possession is very powerful; it crystallizes attachment to the self and to what is "mine." We feel repulsion for what harms us, and this repulsion will change into hatred, then into a disturbed mind, harmful words, violence. These negative emotions are the cause of bad health. Medical studies have shown that people who, in the language of everyday life, use the words "I," "me," or "mine" the most are more subject than others to cardiac diseases. At the root of negative emotions, then, we find the self and a belief in the solidity of things. We have to try to dissipate this belief on ever subtler levels.

Training our emotional life represents a labor of many decades to remedy the negative feelings that have become the normal state of our mind. For we have never tried to learn who we really are. The reification of the self and of phenomena creates a division between subject and object. When we dissipate belief in the reality of the self and the world, we discover that wisdom itself is without any inherent existence. Obviously, that corresponds to an advanced stage on the path.

———

The Dalai Lama has experienced the words of the Buddha, who invites his disciples to examine the scriptures like a goldsmith testing gold. In his teachings, the Dalai Lama transmits the pure gold of his practice through the overabundance of his heart. He sometimes sheds tears when he describes the power of the mind of Enlightenment, which cherishes others more than itself, or else he bursts out laughing when he mentions human naïveté and shortcomings. His tears and his spontaneous laughter are teachings within the teaching, reminding us of the incarnate dimension of wisdom.

In the mirror of the Dalai Lama's limitless generosity, we have a chance to evaluate the path of our life. For it is the very parameters of our relationship to the world that the spiritual master calls into question. What reality should we assign to what we take as "reality"? The reasoning of analytic investigation strips the layers away and deconstructs the person who says "I," "my," "mine," or "me," thereby appropriating the experience of awareness and of the perceptible world. In the land of Descartes, it suddenly seems presumptuous indeed to assert, "I think, therefore I am."

The teaching of Tibetan masters calls such certainties into question: "Your present face is not you," Lama Yeshe writes.

Your bones and flesh are not you. Neither your blood, your muscles, nor any other part of your body is the essence of who you are. . . . Our gross physical body is not the only body we possess. . . . Within the confines of our ordinary physical form exists a subtler conscious body, so called because it is intimately connected with deep levels of consciousness. It is from these subtler levels that the potential energy of blissful wisdom arises, an energy capable of transforming the quality of our life completely. . . . [It] represents the essence of who we are and what we can become.[6]

Through meditative practice, ordinary identity is overcome by the energy of Enlightenment. Access is given to a level of awareness where appearances no longer manifest without the realization of their interdependence, so that "we" becomes more real than "I." Recognizing that we do not have the cause of our existence inside us and that we depend on others for our survival is the first step that allows us to appreciate the essential generosity of life. Buddhist analysis of reality leads us to understand that everything is connected and that compassion is our true nature.

The Dalai Lama often compares religions to medicine, adding that different treatments are necessary to cure different diseases. But all religions are the same in that they all prescribe altruism. Why? Because loving-kindness represents the fundamental health that corresponds to the true nature of reality. Egocentric attitudes, harmful to ourselves and others, go against the truth of life and human beings. They stem from ignorance and lead to mental deviancies that need to be remedied. Wisdom, perceiving reality as it is, represents the supreme remedy of altruism. It is by following this reasoning that the Dalai Lama can assert: "I call love and compassion a universal religion. That is my religion."

Now we can understand that by presenting himself as a human being, the Dalai Lama means that he has effected a process of inner transformation that allows him to recognize the participatory reality of life and to experience its basic goodness. But according to the law of reciprocity associated with the principle of interdependence, we are part of the world as much as the world is part of us.

Whoever transforms himself, transforms the world.

Transforming
the World

I Call for a Spiritual Revolution

We can do without religion,
but not without spirituality

As a Tibetan monk, I was brought up to respect Buddhist principles. My entire way of thinking was shaped by the fact that I am a disciple of the Buddha, but I have wanted to go beyond the borders of my faith to clarify certain universal principles, with the aim of helping everyone find happiness.

It seems important to me to distinguish between religion and spirituality. Religion implies a system of beliefs based on metaphysical foundations, along with the teaching of dogmas, rituals, or prayers. Spirituality, however, corresponds to the development of human qualities such as love, compassion, patience, tolerance, forgiveness, or a sense of responsibility. These inner qualities, which are a source of happiness for oneself and for others, are independent of any religion. That is why I have sometimes stated that one can do without religion, but not without spirituality. And an altruistic motivation is the unifying element of the qualities that I define as *spiritual*.

Spiritual revolution and
ethical revolution

SPIRITUALITY, in my view, consists of transforming the mind. The best way to transform it is to get it used to thinking in a more altruistic way. So ethics is the basis for a secular spirituality for everyone, one that is not limited to a group of believers in one religion or another.

The spiritual revolution that I advocate is not a religious revolution. It corresponds to an ethical reorientation of our attitude, since it is a question of learning to take the aspirations of others into account as much as our own.

The spiritual revolution I advocate does not depend on external conditions linked to material progress or technology. It is born from within, motivated by the profound desire to transform oneself in order to become a better human being.

People may object that a spiritual revolution cannot solve the problems of the contemporary world. They might add that, on the social level, violence, alcoholism, drugs, or the loss of family values should be dealt with on their own ground through specific measures. But we know that more love and compassion would limit the extent and gravity of these problems. Wouldn't it be better to approach them and treat them like problems of a spiritual order?

I am not claiming that such problems will instantly disappear, but I do say that by reducing them to the social sphere and by neglecting their spiritual dimension, we aren't giving ourselves the means to resolve them in a lasting way. Spirituality, when understood as the development of fundamental human values, has every chance to improve the life of our communities.

The sickness of duality

IT IS IMPORTANT TO BECOME AWARE of interdependence by realizing that a phenomenon occurs owing to multiple causes and conditions. Reducing it to one single factor would lead to a fragmentation of reality. Awareness of interdependence eventually brings about a lessening of violence. All the more so because when one places oneself in a wider context, one becomes less vulnerable to external circumstances and acquires a healthier judgment. Nonviolence is not limited to an absence of violence, for it is a matter of an active attitude, motivated by the wish to do others good. It is equivalent to altruism.

Selfless love is often misunderstood. It is not a question of neglecting oneself for others' benefit. In fact, when you benefit others, you benefit yourself because of the principle of interdependence. I want to stress the importance of enlarging your mind and bringing the sufferings of others onto yourself. Altruism changes our temperament, our humor, and our perceptions and allows us to develop a more serene, more even temperament. The opposite of altruism makes us vulnerable to external circumstances.

Egocentrism is against nature, for it ignores interdependence. It is an attitude that closes all the doors, whereas altruism develops profound vision. We should develop the feeling of belonging to a large human family. The causes and conditions of our future are largely in our hands.

The disregard of interdependence by Westerners

GENERALLY, I HAVE BEEN very impressed by Western society; I especially admire its energy, its creativity, and its hunger for knowledge. Still, a certain number of elements in the Western way of life seem worrisome to me. I have noticed, for example, how ready people are to think of everything as completely *white* or completely *black,* as either *this* or *that,* ignoring the reality of interdependence and relativism. They have a tendency to lose sight of the gray zones between opinions.

Another one of my observations is that there are many people in the West who live very comfortably in large cities, while still remaining isolated from the large mass of humanity. It is surprising that with such material ease and with thousands of brothers and sisters as neighbors, such a large number of people can show real affection only for their cats and dogs. In my view, that denotes a lack of spiritual values. Part of the problem might be the intense competition—a source of fear and profound insecurity—involved in living in these countries.

Humanity is *one*

THE HUMAN COMMUNITY has reached a critical point in its history. The world today forces us to accept that humanity is *one*. In the past, the various communities could allow themselves to think that they were separate. But today, as the recent tragic events in the United States have shown,[7] what happens in one country affects many other countries. The world is becoming more and more interdependent. In the context of this new interdependence, self-interest requires us to take into account the interests of others. Without understanding and promoting the sense of our universal responsibility, our future itself is threatened. I firmly believe that we must cultivate a greater sense of universal responsibility. We must learn how to work not just for ourselves, our family, or our nation, but for the good of humanity. Universal responsibility is the best possible basis to ensure our personal happiness and world peace. It implies that everyone be given equal access to natural resources, by protecting the environment for future generations. Many problems in the world arise because we have lost sight of the basic *humanity* that unites all members

family. We tend to forget that despite the diversity of
religion, culture, language, and ideology, we all have an equal
and fundamental right to peace and happiness. Each one of us wants
to be happy and not to suffer. However, although we theoretically
praise pluralism, unfortunately we often fail to put it into practice. In
fact, our inability to embrace diversity has become a major source of
conflict among peoples.[8]

Interdependence is a law of nature

INTERDEPENDENCE is a fundamental law of nature. It concerns more than just the more evolved forms of life, for even the smallest insects are social beings who, without the slightest religion, law, or education, survive thanks to mutual cooperation, based on an innate recognition of their interrelatedness. The myriad forms of life as well as the subtlest levels of material phenomena are governed by interdependence. All phenomena in the planet we live on, from the oceans to the clouds, the forests, and the flowers that surround us, survive in dependence according to subtle forms of energy. Without appropriate interaction, they disintegrate and disappear.

A sense of responsibility is
born from compassion

I N TIBET WE SAY that many illnesses can be cured exclusively by the remedy of love and compassion. These qualities are the ultimate source of happiness, and we need them in our innermost being.

Unfortunately, love and compassion have been excluded from too many areas of social interaction, for too long a time. Confined to the private sphere of the family, their public expression is deemed embarrassing or even naive. This is tragic, for in my opinion the expression of compassion, far from being a mark of idealism cut off from reality, is the most effective way to serve the interests of others as well as our own.

A mind dedicated to compassion is like an overflowing reservoir: it is a constant source of energy, determination, and goodness. You could compare compassion to a seed. If you cultivate it, it makes an abundance of other excellent qualities blossom, such as forgiveness, tolerance, inner strength, and confidence, allowing us to conquer fear and anxiety. The compassionate mind is like an elixir: it has the strength to turn adverse situations into beneficial circumstances. Therefore, we shouldn't limit our expression of love and compassion just to our family and friends. Nor is compassion the sole responsibility of the clergy and health care and social workers. It necessarily concerns all domains of the human community.

When a conflict arises in the field of politics, business, or religion, the altruistic approach is often the only possible solution. Sometimes the arguments used as means of reconciliation are themselves the cause of the problem. In such a case, when a solution seems impossible, both parties should remember the basic human nature they have in common. That will help them find a way out of the impasse, and in the long run everyone can reach his goal more easily. It is very likely that no one will be completely satisfied, but if both sides make concessions, at least the danger of the conflict degenerating will be defused. We all know that such compromises are the best way to solve problems. So why don't we use them more often?

When I consider the lack of cooperation in society, I tell myself it is due to ignorance of our interdependent nature. I am often moved by little insects, like bees. The laws of nature dictate that they work together in order to survive, since they are endowed with an instinctive sense of social responsibility. They have no constitution, laws, police, religion, or moral education, but they faithfully work together because of their nature. There are times when they might fight, but in general the entire colony survives thanks to cooperation. Human beings have constitutions, elaborate legal systems and police forces, religions, remarkable intelligence, and hearts endowed with the ability to love. But despite these extraordinary qualities, in actual practice we lag behind the smallest of insects. In some ways, I feel that we are poorer than the bees.

Although we are social animals, forced to live together, we lack a sense of responsibility toward our fellow humans. Does the fault lie in the basic structures of family and society? In the facilities produced by science and technology? I don't think so.

I think that despite the rapid advances that civilization has made over the past century, the immediate cause of our present situation is exclusively privileging material progress above all else. We have thrown ourselves so frantically into its pursuit that we have neglected to pay attention to the essential human needs of love, kindness, cooperation, and caring. It is clear to me that an authentic sense of responsibility can emerge only if we develop compassion. Only a spontaneous feeling of empathy toward others can motivate us to act on their behalf.

War is an anachronism

WAR, or any form of organized combat, developed alongside civilization and seems to be part of history and of the human temperament.

However, the world is changing, and we have understood that we cannot solve human problems with weapons. The disputes that result from differences of opinion should be settled gradually through dialogue.

Obviously, wars produce conquerors and conquered, but only temporarily. The victories or defeats resulting from wars cannot last very long. Moreover, our world has become so interdependent that the defeat of one country has repercussions throughout the rest of the world and leads directly or indirectly to suffering and loss for each one of us.

Today, in such an interdependent world, the concept of war seems anachronistic, stemming from outmoded attitudes. We are always talking about reform and change. Many traditions from the past are no longer adapted to the present and are even counterproductive and have thus been relegated to the dustbins of history. War should also be consigned to the dustbins of history.

Unfortunately, although we've entered the twenty-first century, we haven't made a clean break with past habits: I refer to the belief that we can solve problems with weapons. It is because of this idea that the world continues to experience all sorts of difficulties. But what should we do? What is to be done when the major world powers have already made their decisions? We can wish for a gradual end to the tradition of wars.

Naturally, one doesn't easily put an end to the militaristic tradition. But think about it. If there is carnage, the men in power or the leaders will have safe shelters; they will escape the painful consequences by finding asylum. But what will happen to the poor people, the children, the old, the sick? They are the ones who will have to bear the brunt.

When weapons speak, they create death and destruction without distinguishing between the innocent and the guilty. The missile launched by the enemy does not respect the innocent, the poor, the defenseless—the very people deserving of compassion. As a result, the real losers are the ones who lead a simple life.

The only positive point: those benevolent organizations that bring medical and humanitarian aid and intervene in regions torn apart by conflicts. The development of these organizations is a victory of the heart in the modern era.

Let us hope and pray that there is no war at all, if possible. If a war breaks out, let us pray that there is the least possible carnage and suffering. I do not know if our prayers will bring any aid, in concrete terms, but it is all we can do for now.

———————

This declaration was made in Dharamsala on March 11, 2003, when threats of war in Iraq were looming. Six months later, in October 2003, during teachings given in Paris, the Dalai Lama noted that, in the accusations made against Iraq's leader, Saddam Hussein, no mention was made of the fact that the dictator's weapons had been made with the use of Western technology. He pointed out that the greed of the weapons-trafficking governments should be denounced along with the bloodthirsty tyrant.

In January 2009 in Sarnath, the Dalai Lama recalled this example in order to illustrate interdependence and the necessity of every individual becoming aware of the universal responsibility we all share and recognizing that the smallest action affects the world.

Everyone must assume a share
of universal responsibility

I DON'T BELIEVE IN THE CREATION of mass movements or in ideologies. And I do not appreciate the fashion of creating an organization in order to promote one idea or another, which implies that one small group is solely responsible for carrying out a given project, to the exclusion of everyone else. In the present circumstances, no one should assume that someone else will solve his problems. Everyone must assume his own share of universal responsibility. This way, as the number of concerned, responsible individuals increases— first dozens, then hundreds, then thousands and even hundreds of thousands—the general atmosphere will be improved.[9]

The Dalai Lama does not subscribe to ideologies that distance individuals from the awareness necessary to assume their humanity fully. The freshness of his position consists in centering the resolution of problems on the individual and on ethics.

Compassion is the truth of the human being, and it comes about by developing an altruistic attitude on the individual level. On a global level, compassion leads to developing universal responsibility. During a time of globalized history and worldwide civilization, we all assume our share of universal responsibility wherever we live. Every individual action has widespread repercussions. Every person's field of action has become global, with individual freedom conferring duties as well as rights.

As a result of our interdependence, impoverishing a country, a people, or a culture deprives humanity of an irreplaceable share of its rich diversity.

An attack on the basic rights of one human individual becomes an attack on the dignity of all.

What's more, according to the Dalai Lama, awareness of universal responsibility should extend to the realm of the sciences. For human dignity is flouted not just by the policies of repressive and totalitarian governments or by armed conflicts. The moral integrity of human beings has for decades been facing a new challenge that becomes even more pressing as science and technology continue to make new advances. These disciplines now have the power to manipulate the actual genetic codes of life.

To allow science to assume its responsibility in the service of the human individual, the Dalai Lama has been engaged in a dialogue with scholars of worldwide renown. On the basis of Buddhism, understood as a science of the mind, he has emphasized the convergences between his own contemplative tradition and the contemporary neurosciences. As a result of this dialogue, a definition of ethical principles applicable to the scientific realm has emerged, along with innovative research prospects.

My Dialogue with the Sciences

Why is a Buddhist monk interested in science?

IN RECENT DECADES, we have witnessed prodigious advances in the scientific understanding of the human brain and body, and along with new developments in genetics, the investigation of the functioning of the living organism has now reached the very subtle level of individual genes. Heretofore undreamt-of possibilities for manipulating the very codes of the human being have resulted from this. An entirely new form of reality is now emerging for humanity.

Today the question of the interface between science and humanity is no longer just an academic matter but should assume a sense of urgency for all those who are concerned with the fate of humanity. So it seems to me that a dialogue between the neurosciences and society could help deepen our basic understanding of what it means to be human by defining the responsibilities toward nature that we share with other sentient beings. I am happy to note that, as part of this wider interface, some neuroscientists are showing more and more interest in engaging in deeper conversations with the contemplative disciplines of Buddhism.

I began by approaching the sciences with the curiosity of an insatiable boy who grew up in Tibet. Then I gradually became aware of the colossal importance of science and technology in understanding the contemporary world. Not only did I try to grasp scientific concepts, but I also wanted to explore the wider implications of the recent advances in science for the field of human knowledge and technological ability. The specific realms of science that I have explored over the years are subatomic physics, cosmology, biology, and psychology. The limited understanding I acquired in these disciplines I owe to the hours that Carl von Weizsäcker and the late David Bohm generously shared with me. I am profoundly grateful to them, and I regard them as my professors of quantum mechanics. In biology and the neurosciences, my teachers were Robert Livingstone and Francisco Varela, both now deceased. I also owe a lot to the many eminent scholars with whom I have had the privilege of talking under the auspices of the institute that initiated the "Mind and Life" conferences at my residence in Dharamsala, India, in 1987. These dialogues continued over time, and we have concluded the last one here, in Washington, this week.

I understand that many of you are wondering, "Why is a Buddhist monk so interested in science? What connection can there be between modern science and Buddhism, an ancient Indian philosophical and spiritual tradition? What sort of benefit can a discipline such as the neurosciences gain by engaging in a dialogue with the contemplative Buddhist tradition?"

Although our tradition and contemporary science have evolved from different historical, intellectual, and cultural roots, I believe that at bottom they share a similar philosophical outlook and methodology. On the philosophical level, Buddhism and modern science both question any notion of the absolute, whether it presents itself as a transcendent being, an eternal, unchanging principle, such as the soul, or as a fundamental substratum of reality. Buddhism and science prefer to take into account the evolution and emergence of the cosmos and of life, in terms of complex interrelations stemming from the natural law of causality.

As for their methodology, both traditions insist on the role of empiricism. Thus, in Buddhist investigation, out of the three sources of knowledge—experience, reason, and testimony—it is experiential proof that takes precedence, with reason coming second and testimony last. That means that, in Buddhist questioning of reality, at least in principle, empirical proof holds sway over scriptural authority, no matter how venerated a scripture may be. Even in the case of knowledge deduced by reasoning or inference, its validity must ultimately be confirmed by factual experience.

Because of this methodological viewpoint, I have often pointed out to my Buddhist colleagues that the empirically verified discoveries made by modern astronomy should compel us to modify and, in some cases, reject many aspects of traditional cosmology expounded in ancient religious treatises.

Since the primary motive of Buddhist analysis of reality is a fundamental quest to overcome suffering and perfect the human condition, the primary orientation of our investigative tradition has been to understand the human mind and the different ways it functions. The presupposition is that by acquiring a more profound understanding of the psyche, we will find the way to transform our thoughts, emotions, and their underlying propensities so as to define a healthier, more satisfying way of living.

In such a context, Buddhist tradition has provided an exhaustive classification of mental states, as well as contemplative methods aimed at refining certain qualities of the mind. An authentic exchange has been established between the accumulated knowledge and experience of Buddhism and modern science on the great questions dealing with the human mind, from cognition and the emotions to the understanding of the brain's inherent capacity for transformation. This dialogue has turned out to be profoundly interesting and beneficial. For my part, I have drawn much from my conversations with neuroscientists and psychologists when we discussed the nature and role of positive and negative emotions, of attention, imagery, and cerebral plasticity. The indisputable proofs furnished by the neurosciences and medicine on the crucial role of affection transmitted by simple physical touch in regards to the physical development of a newborn infant's brain during the first weeks of life confirm the close link between compassion and the human quest for happiness.[10]

Humanity is at a crossroads

I AM CONVINCED THAT a close collaboration between our two investigative traditions, Buddhism and science, can contribute significantly to developing an understanding of the complex inner world of subjective experience that we call *the mind*. The benefits of such a collaboration are already being demonstrated. According to preliminary reports, the effects of training the mind, such as simple mindfulness practiced on a regular basis or development of compassion in the Buddhist sense, provoke observable changes in the zones of the brain related to positive mental states. These changes have been measured, and recent discoveries in the neurosciences have demonstrated the internal plasticity of the brain, in terms of both synaptic connections and the birth of new neurons due to external stimuli such as voluntary physical exercise or an enriched environment.

The Buddhist contemplative tradition can help extend this field of scientific research by offering certain forms of mind training associated with cerebral plasticity. If it is proven, as Buddhist tradition maintains, that mental practice can effect observable synaptic and neural changes in the brain, this could have far-reaching implications. The repercussions of such research will not be limited to the development of our knowledge of the human brain. Perhaps more importantly, they could contribute to our understanding of education and mental health. Similarly, if, as Buddhist tradition claims, the deliberate practice of compassion can bring about a radical change in an individual's outlook, leading to a greater empathy for others, this could have important consequences for society in general.

Finally, I believe that collaboration between the neurosciences and the contemplative tradition of Buddhism can shed a new light on the question of the interface between ethics and the neurosciences, which is of vital importance. Whatever we might think about the relationship between ethics and science, in actual practice, science has evolved first as an empirical, morally neutral discipline. It has come to be regarded mainly as a method of investigation that provides a detailed knowledge of the empirical world and the underlying laws of nature.

From a purely scientific standpoint, the creation of nuclear weapons represents a remarkable achievement. However, since these weapons have the power to inflict an immense amount of suffering by causing death and massive destruction, we regard this achievement as an aberration of science.

It is ethical evaluation that allows us to determine what is positive or negative in the sciences. Until recently, it would seem that ethics and science have been successfully compartmentalized, with the understanding that the human capacity for moral thinking evolved along with knowledge. Today, however, I believe that humanity is at a critical crossroads. The radical advances in the neurosciences, and especially in genetics, toward the end of the twentieth century have opened up a new era in human history. We have reached a point where the ethical challenges posed by these advances are immense.

Obviously, our moral thinking has not been able to keep pace with such a rapid development of knowledge and the power it confers. Yet the ramifications of these new discoveries and their applications are so far-reaching that our very concept of human nature and the preservation of the species are called into question. So it is no longer acceptable to adopt the view that our responsibility as a society is simply to support scientific knowledge and reinforce technological power, leaving open the question of what should be done with them. We must find a way to allow humanitarian and ethical considerations to determine the direction of scientific progress, especially in the life sciences.

By invoking fundamental ethical principles, I am not advocating a fusion between religious ethics and scientific research. I am referring rather to what I call "secular ethics," which includes the key ethical principles such as compassion, tolerance, kindness, and the responsible use of science and power. These principles transcend the boundaries between believers and nonbelievers, as well as those between disciples of different religions. The world in which we live is *one world*. The modern economy, electronic media, international tourism, and environmental problems all remind us on a daily basis how interconnected the present world is. The scientific communities play a vital role in this interconnected world. Science today enjoys society's great respect and trust, much more than my own philosophical and religious discipline does. I appeal to scholars to bring into their professional work the values stemming from the fundamental ethical principles we all share as human beings.[11]

Ethics in the sciences to save life

I SEE AN ENCOURAGING SIGN in the increasing compatibility between science and religion. Throughout all of the nineteenth century and for a large part of the twentieth, there has been profound confusion because of the conflict between these two seemingly contradictory views of the world. Today physics, biology, and psychology have reached such sophisticated levels that many researchers begin by asking the most profound questions about the ultimate nature of the universe and of life—the same questions that are of prime interest in the field of religion. So a real potential for a more unified vision does exist. More particularly, a new concept of the mind and of matter seems to be emerging. Historically, the East was more concerned with understanding the mind and the West was more involved in understanding matter. Now that both have met, these spiritual and material concepts of life can come to harmonize.

We have to renew our commitments to human values in the sciences. Although the main aim of science is to gain ever more knowledge of reality, another of its objectives is to improve the quality of life. Without altruistic motivation, scientists are unable to distinguish between beneficial technologies and harmful, short-term expedients. The damage caused to the environment around us is the most obvious consequence of this confusion. A suitable motivation is even more imperative when it is a question of managing the extraordinary spectrum of new biotechnologies with which we can now manipulate the subtle structures of the living organism. If we don't base these manipulations on an ethical foundation, we risk causing irremediable harm to the delicate web of life.

The Dalai Lama thinks that in our time Buddhism should take on a special responsibility, one derived from the teaching of the Buddha that posits meditation on interdependence as inseparable from the practice of compassion. The concept of interdependence, as it was presented by the Buddha 2,500 years ago and then commented on by the sages of ancient India and Tibet, fits into the vision of the world that stems from general relativity and its subsequent developments. On this subject, the Dalai Lama often quotes Abdul Kalam, whom he calls "the Indian Sakharov." This former president of India, a specialist in nuclear physics, told the Dalai Lama that he had found the essence of quantum uncertainty in the thinking of the Indian sage Nagarjuna, as expressed in these verses paying homage to the Buddha:

> *I bow down to You, who transcend the world,*
> *Versed in the wisdom of absence!*
> *For the good of the world*
> *You suffered for a long time, with great compassion.*
> *You assert that aside from the simple aggregates*
> *No sentient being exists.*
> *However, O Great Sage, You remain constantly*
> *Completely devoted to the welfare of beings.*
> *An existent thing is not produced,*
> *Nor is a nonexistent thing, nor both together.*
> *It is produced neither from itself nor from something else,*
> *Nor from both, so how could there be production?*
> *First of all, it is not logical for an effect to emerge*
> *From a cause that is itself destroyed;*
> *Nor is it produced from a nondestroyed cause.*
> *So You accept a production that is like a dream.*
> *The emergence of effects from a cause*

Through destruction or nondestruction,
This production is like the manifestation of an illusion,
And You taught that this is true for everything.
Whatever is produced in dependence
You maintain is empty,
That it does not exist as an independent entity,
That is what You proclaimed with the lion's roar,
O incomparable Master.
Since You teach the nectar of emptiness
In order to help us abandon all concepts,
You strongly condemned
The act of being attached to this emptiness.
Since phenomena are inert, dependent, and empty,
Similar to an illusion and born from conditions,
You made it known that they lack reality.
Without entering into meditation,
As the Noble Ones have demonstrated,
Can awareness ever do without signs?
Without entering into the absence of signs
There is no Liberation, You declared.
So You presented the absence of sign
Completely in the sutras of the Great Vehicle.
By praising You, O praiseworthy vessel,
Thanks to whatever merits I have obtained,
May all beings, without exception,
Free themselves from enslavement to signs.[12]

The tragedy of September 11, 2001, taught me that we must not separate ethics from progress

DESTRUCTIVE EMOTIONS like anger, fear, or hatred can have devastating effects on the world. When current events offer us a tragic reminder of the destructive power of these emotions, we should ask ourselves how we can control them. Of course, they have always been part of the human condition. Humanity has been grappling with them for thousands of years. But I believe that we should seize this occasion to transform them, thanks especially to a collaboration between religion and the sciences. It is with this idea in mind that starting in 1987 I became involved in a series of dialogues organized by the Mind and Life Institute; I found that while scientific discoveries offer a more profound understanding of fields of knowledge like cosmology, Buddhist explanations can help scholars see their own field of research in a different light.

Our dialogue benefited not just science but also religion. Although Tibetans have a valid knowledge of the inner world, we have remained apart from material progress because of a lack of scientific knowledge. Buddhist teachings insist on the importance of understanding reality; therefore, we should examine how contemporary scientists see the reality discovered by their experiments and their quantifications.

At the beginning of these dialogues, there weren't many Buddhists. I was the only one, working with two translators. But recently we have begun to introduce the study of contemporary sciences in our monasteries, and during recent sessions of dialogue there were about twenty Tibetan monks in the audience.

The aim of these conversations is twofold. One is of an academic nature: developing knowledge. In general, science has represented an extraordinary instrument for understanding the material world, and it has made huge advances in our lifetime, even though many things still remain to be explored. But modern science does not seem to have progressed much with regard to inner experience. On the other hand, Buddhism, an ancient system of Indian thought, testifies to a profound analysis of how the mind functions. For centuries a great number of meditators have conducted what could be called "experiments" in this realm and have obtained significant and sometimes extraordinary results, using all the knowledge available to them. A deeper discussion and joint study carried out by both scientists and Buddhist scholars could be very useful on an academic level in furthering human knowledge.

On another level, if humanity is to survive, happiness and inner peace are essential. Otherwise, the lives of our children and their children risk being unhappy, desperate, and short. The tragedy of September 11, 2001, showed that modern technology and human intelligence, guided by hatred, can lead to immense destruction. Of course, material progress contributes to happiness to a certain extent, and to a comfortable way of life. But that is not enough. To reach a deeper level of happiness, we cannot neglect our inner development. My feeling is that our sense of basic human values must be pursued at the same pace as the recent increase in our material abilities.

It is for this reason that I have encouraged scholars to examine advanced Tibetan meditators in order to determine how their spiritual practice could be more beneficial to others outside the religious context. For it is important to have a better understanding of the world of the mind, of awareness, and of the emotions.

Experiments have already been carried out demonstrating that meditators can reach a state of inner peace and maintain it, even in difficult circumstances. The results prove that they are happier, less subject to destructive emotions, and more receptive to the feelings of others. Contemplative methods are not just useful but inexpensive! You don't have to buy anything or make anything in a factory. You don't need medications or injections.

The question that arises is how to share the benefit of these results with non-Buddhists. For it is a matter of not limiting this investigation either to Buddhism or to any other religion, but of understanding better the potential of the human mind. Spiritual methods are at our disposal, but we must make them accessible to the majority who aren't interested in spirituality. That is the only way they will have the greatest impact.

Such an initiative is important because science and technology alone cannot solve all our problems. We must join material progress with the inner development of the human values of compassion, tolerance, forgiveness, moderation, and self-discipline.[13]

In approaching the tragedy of September 11, 2001, as a "spiritual" problem, the Dalai Lama denounces the absence of a code of ethics in scientific research. As a result of this absence, major actions conceived by the human mind turn against human beings, whether in the terrorist attack against the twin towers of the World Trade Center, in uncontrollable genetic experiments, or in the accelerated degradation of the environment that threatens future generations. As a Buddhist monk, the Dalai Lama states that on this question too, spirituality, understood as a return to essential human values, is the key to our survival.

∽ **5** ∽

Taking Care of the Earth

Our Ecological Responsibility

As a child, I learned from my teachers to take care of the environment

As a little boy, when I was studying Buddhism, I was taught to take care of nature, since the practice of nonviolence applies not just to human beings but to all sentient beings. Everything that is animate possesses consciousness. Wherever there is consciousness, there are feelings like pain, pleasure, and joy. No sentient being wants to suffer. On the contrary, all beings search for happiness. In Buddhist practice, we are so used to this idea of nonviolence and to the wish to put an end to all suffering that we are careful not to attack or destroy life unwittingly. Obviously, we do not believe that the trees or flowers have a mind, but we treat them with respect. So we assume a sense of universal responsibility toward humanity and nature.

Our belief in reincarnation explains our concern for the future. If you think you are going to be reborn, you make it your duty to protect certain things so that, in the future, your incarnation will profit from it. Even though you could be reborn on another planet, the idea of reincarnation motivates you to take care of the Earth and of future generations.

In the West, when we speak of "humanity," we are usually referring merely to the present generation. The humanity of the past no longer exists. The humanity of the future, like death, does not yet exist. From a Western standpoint, we are concerned with the practical aspect of things, solely for the present generation.

Tibetan feelings toward nature stem from our customs in general and not just from Buddhism. If you take the example of Buddhism in Japan or Thailand, in environments different from our own, the culture and behavior are not the same. Tibet's natural environment, which is like no other, has had a strong influence on us. Tibetans do not live on a small overpopulated island. Throughout history we did not worry about our vast, sparsely populated territory, or about our distant neighbors. We did not have the feeling of being oppressed, unlike many other communities.

It is perfectly possible to practice the essence of a faith or a culture without associating it with a religion. Our Tibetan culture, although largely inspired by Buddhism, does not draw all its philosophy from it. Once I suggested to an organization aiding Tibetan refugees that it would be interesting to study how much our people have been shaped by their traditional mode of life. What are the factors that make Tibetans calm and good-natured? People always look for the answer in our religion, which is unique, forgetting that our environment is also unique.

The protection of nature is not necessarily a sacred activity, and it does not always require compassion. As Buddhists, we are compassionate toward all sentient beings, but not necessarily toward each stone, tree, or habitation. Most of us take care of our own house, without feeling any compassion for it. Similarly, our planet is our house, and we should maintain it with care, to ensure our happiness and the happiness of our children, of our friends, and of all the sentient beings who share this great dwelling place. If we think of our planet as our house or our "mother," our *Mother Earth*, we will necessarily take care of it.

Today we understand that the future of humanity depends on our planet, whose future depends on humanity. But that has not always been so clear. Until now, our Mother Earth has been able to tolerate our neglect. Today, however, human behavior, the population, and technology have reached such a degree that our Mother Earth can no longer accept it in silence. "My children are behaving badly," she warns to make us realize that there are boundaries that should not be passed.

As Tibetan Buddhists, we advocate temperance, which is not unconnected to the environment, since we do not consume anything immoderately. We set limits on our habits of consumption, and we appreciate a simple, responsible way of life. Our relationship to the environment has always been special. Our ancient scriptures speak of the vessel and its contents. The world is the *vessel*, our house, and we, the living, are its *contents*.

The result of this is a special relationship to nature, since, without the container, the contents cannot be contained. It is not at all reprehensible for humans to use natural resources to serve their needs, but we should not exploit nature beyond what is strictly necessary. It is essential to reexamine from an ethical standpoint the share we have received, the share for which we are all responsible, and the share we are going to hand down to future generations. Obviously, our generation is going through a critical stage. We have access to forms of global communication, and yet conflicts occur more often than dialogues to build peace. The wonders of science and technology coexist along with many tragedies like world hunger and the extinction of certain forms of life. We devote ourselves to space exploration when the oceans, seas, and freshwater resources are becoming more and more polluted. It is possible that the peoples of the Earth, the animals, plants, insects, and even microorganisms will be unknown to future generations. We must act before it is too late.

The Tibet of my childhood, paradise of wildlife

THE TIBET I GREW UP IN was a wildlife paradise. Even in Lhasa one did not feel in any way cut off from the natural world. In my rooms at the top of the Potala, the winter palace of the Dalai Lamas, I spent countless hours as a child studying the behavior of the red-beaked *khyungkar*, which nested in the crevices of its walls. And behind the Norbulingka, the summer palace, I often saw pairs of *trung trung* (Japanese black-necked cranes), birds which are for me the epitome of elegance and grace, that lived in the marshlands there. Not to mention the crowning glory of Tibetan fauna: the bears and mountain foxes, the *chanku* (wolves), *sazik* (the beautiful snow leopard), the gentle-faced giant panda, which is native to the border area between Tibet and China, and the *sik* (lynx), which struck terror into the hearts of the nomad farmers.

Sadly, this profusion of wildlife is no longer to be found. Without exception, every Tibetan I have spoken with who has been back to visit Tibet after an absence of forty or fifty years has reported on the striking absence of wildlife. Before, wild animals would often come close to the house; today they are hardly anywhere to be seen.[14]

The Dalai Lama remembers his childhood fascination with different animals, especially the ones he saw during the three-month journey across Tibet to be enthroned in Lhasa. The Tibetan government officially protected animal life, posting proclamations every year declaring that "rich or poor, no one may harm or do violence to the creatures of the land and water." But since the Chinese occupation, development of the land and hunting and fishing have steadily reduced the presence of wildlife. Animals have been hunted for their fur, their hide, their wool, and their organs, and many species are now extinct or endangered.

In Tibet the mountains have become bald as monks' heads

ECOLOGICAL PROBLEMS ARE NEW TO ME. In Tibet we used to think that nature was pure. We never asked ourselves if it was all right to drink the water from a river. But the situation has changed during our exile in India or other countries. Switzerland, for instance, is a magnificent, impressive land. But its inhabitants tell us, "Don't drink the water from this stream; it's polluted!" So little by little, Tibetans learned and realized that certain things are dirty and unusable. Actually, when we settled in India, many of us fell sick and had stomach problems because we had drunk polluted water. It is through experience and meeting experts that we learned about ecology.

Tibet is a large country with a vast territory at a high altitude and with a cold, dry climate. These conditions probably provided the environment with a natural form of protection by keeping it clean and cool. In the meadows in the north, in the mineral zones, in the forests and river valleys, there were many wild animals, fish, and birds.

Once I was told a strange thing. The Chinese who settled in Tibet after 1959 were farmers who built roads and liked meat very much. They used to go duck hunting, buttoned up in their army uniforms or in Chinese clothes that alarmed the birds so they flew far away. Eventually, these hunters resorted to wearing Tibetan clothes. This is a true story! This happened especially during the 1970s and 1980s, at a time when there were still a large number of birds.

Recently, a few thousand Tibetans went back to their birthplace in Tibet. They all say the same thing. They say that forty or fifty years earlier, immense forests covered their native land. Today the mountains have become bald as monks' heads. There are no more tall trees, and sometimes even the roots have been dug up and taken away. That is the present situation. In the past one would see large herds of wild animals, but now there are almost none left.

Large-scale deforestation in Tibet is distressing. It is not just regrettable for the natural sites that have lost their beauty, but also for the inhabitants who find it hard to find wood to heat their houses. This is a relatively minor point compared to the grave consequences of deforestation viewed from a wider perspective.

The majority of Tibet comprises arid zones at high altitudes. Thus, the earth there needs more time to renew itself than in lower-altitude regions with a humid climate. Negative effects are felt for a longer period of time. Moreover, the rivers that irrigate most of Asia, including Pakistan, India, China, Vietnam, Laos, and Cambodia—the Yellow River, the Brahmaputra, the Yangtze, the Salween, and the Mekong—all originate in Tibet. Pollution of the rivers has catastrophic repercussions for the countries downstream. Yet it is at their source that both widespread deforestation and drilling for mines are occurring.

According to Chinese statistics, there are 126 types of minerals in Tibet. When these resources were discovered, the Chinese exploited them intensively, taking no protective measures for the environment, so that deforestation and mining sites are causing more and more floods in the lowlands of Tibet.

According to climatologists, the deforestation of the Tibetan plateau will change the impact of cosmic radiation on ice (since forests absorb more solar radiation) and that will affect the monsoon, not just in Tibet but in neighboring regions. So it is of prime importance to preserve the very fragile environment of the high plateau. Unfortunately, in the Communist world, as we've seen in countries like the former Soviet Union, Poland, and the former East Germany, many problems of pollution were caused by negligence. Factory production was increased with no care taken to avoid harming the environment. The same situation is being repeated in the People's Republic of China. In the 1970s and 1980s, no one paid any attention to the pollution, but since then there has been a rise in consciousness. I think the previous situations arose from ignorance.

In Tibet it seems that, when it comes to the environment, Chinese officials are applying discriminatory measures: negligence seems to be occurring in regions inhabited by certain ethnic groups. A Tibetan who comes from the region of Dingri in the south of Tibet told me about a river from which villagers drew their drinking water. The Chinese in the People's Liberation Army living in the area had been instructed not to drink it, but no one informed the Tibetans of the risks linked to its consumption. So they continue to drink it. This shows that Chinese disregard continues and is not due to a lack of information but to other reasons.

The lives of six million Tibetans are in grave danger because of pollution. Children are already suffering from diseases linked to air pollution. There is an immense amount of suffering and anguish that isn't heard about abroad but is confined to the secrecy of humble homes. It is in the name of innocent people that I speak.[15]

A policy of systematic deforestation, done for China's profit, has deprived Tibet of half its forests. The consequences, denounced by the Dalai Lama, are devastating and affect all of Asia. During the floods of the Yangtze that caused a national catastrophe in China in August 1998, the central government admitted that the tragedy was caused by the massive deforestation around the river's sources in the Tibetan province of Kham. At present, quotas have been established to protect the forests, but they are rarely respected. In these conditions, the vegetation no longer regenerates, and the desertification of the Tibetan plateau continues, reducing the output of the main rivers by one-quarter. Four hundred large cities in China now suffer from a dearth of water, and in the countryside the harvests are affected by a lack of irrigation.

As the Dalai Lama reminds us, the subsoil of the high Tibetan plateau is rich in minerals, which are many and diverse. This abundance of mining resources was one of the main reasons for the Chinese invasion of 1949. The Chinese continue to exploit large deposits of uranium, chrome, gold, lithium, borax, iron, and silver. Oil and natural gas reserves in the region of Tsaidam constitute a prime energy supply for China's accelerated industrialization.

Mining carried out with no concern for the environment has disastrous consequences for the soil and the phreatic layer, which today are polluted by the toxic waste used in extraction. Far from putting a stop to these practices, Chinese industrialists are trying to increase them by attracting foreign investors. The Tibetans who had the courage to protest the destruction of the environment were rewarded with torture and long prison sentences.

Reflections of a Buddhist monk
on our ecological responsibility

OVER THE COURSE of my many journeys throughout the world, to rich and poor countries, to the East and the West, I have seen people who enjoy every form of pleasure and other people who are suffering. Advances in science and technology seem to end up only in a one-sided and quantitative improvement of development that ought to represent more than just a few additional houses in new cities. And ecological balance, the basis of our life on Earth, has been greatly affected.

In the past, the Tibetan people lived a happy life, in a nature preserved from all pollution. Today, everywhere in the world, including Tibet, ecological degradation is quickly catching up to us. I am completely convinced that if we don't make a concentrated effort together, and if we fail to realize our universal responsibility, we will witness the gradual destruction of fragile ecosystems, the sources of our survival, which will lead to the irreversible and irrevocable degradation of Planet Earth.

I composed these verses to express my profound concern and to solicit the efforts of all people to heal our environment and put an end to its degradation.

O Lord Tathagata,[16] born in the tree of the Ikshvaku lineage,[17]
O Unparalleled One who sees the all-pervasive interdependence
Between environment and sentient beings,

Samsara and nirvana, animate and inanimate,
O You who teach in this world from compassion,
Confer on us Your loving-kindness!
O Savior, whom we invoke with the name Avalokiteshvara,[18]
Because You embody the compassion of all the Buddhas,
We pray to You to make our minds ripen and bear fruit,
So that we can observe reality without illusion.
Stubborn self-centeredness, which has impregnated our minds
Since beginningless time,
Contaminates, soils, and pollutes the environment
Created by the shared karma of all sentient beings.
Lakes and pools have lost their clarity and freshness.
The atmosphere is poisoned.
The heavenly canopy of nature, rising into the burning
    firmament,
Has shattered, and sentient beings
Are suffering from diseases heretofore unknown.
Mountains with eternal snows, resplendent with glory,
Are bending and collapsing, reduced to water.
The majestic oceans are overflowing their age-old limits
And drowning islands.
Fire, water, and wind expose us to countless dangers.
Oppressive heat is drying out our luxuriant forests,
Lashing our world with unprecedented storms,
While the oceans are yielding their salt to the elements.
Although peoples do not lack wealth,
They cannot buy themselves the luxury of breathing pure air.
Rain showers and streams no longer clean anything
But become inert, powerless liquids.
Human beings and living organisms, countless in number,

Inhabiting the realms of water and earth,

Are tottering beneath the yoke of physical pain

Caused by malignant ailments.

Their minds are weakened by laziness, stupidity, and ignorance.

The joys of the body and mind have gone far, far away.

We are uselessly soiling

The beautiful bosom of our Mother Earth,

Destroying her trees to serve our short-term greed,

So that fertile soil becomes sterile desert.

The interdependent nature of the external environment

And the internal world of human beings,

As described in the Tantras[19]

And in treatises on medicine and astronomy,

Has been verified by present experience.

The earth is the house of living beings;

It is equable and impartial to animate and inanimate alike.

Thus spoke the Buddha with a voice that speaks the truth,

Taking the great Earth as his witness.

Just as a noble being recognizes the kindness of a wise mother

And shows gratitude to her,

So we should treat with affection and thoughtfulness

The Earth, our universal mother,

Who gives everyone equal nourishment.

Let us abandon waste and pollution

Of the clean, clear nature of the four elements,

And let us stop destroying the well-being of peoples!

Let us devote ourselves on the contrary to actions that benefit
    everyone!

Buddha, the Great Sage, was born beneath a tree,

Then sat beneath a tree to complete his Enlightenment,

After having conquered his passions.

And it is beneath two trees that he passed into nirvana.

In truth, the Buddha held trees in high esteem.

The place where the emanation of Manjushri,

Lama Tsongkhapa,[20] caused his body to be born,

Is marked by a sandalwood tree

Whose leaves by the hundreds of thousands bear the effigy of
  the Buddha.

Is it not well known that certain transcendent deities,

Eminent divinities and spirits of place,

Establish their residence in trees?

Flowering trees clean the wind

And let us breathe an air that regenerates life.

They charm the eyes and calm the mind.

Their shade creates a welcoming place of rest.

In the Vinaya,[21] the Buddha advises monks

To care for fragile trees.

This teaching teaches us that it is virtuous

To plant trees and protect their growth.

The Buddha forbids monks to cut down

Or to have others cut down living plants,

To destroy seeds or soil the green, fresh grass.

Should that not inspire in us

Love and protection for our environment?

It is said that, in the heavenly realms,

Trees emanate from the blessings of the Buddha

And echo his words,

Expressing his fundamental teaching of impermanence.

It is trees that bring rain

And retain the essence of the soil's fertility.

The Kalpataru,[22] the wish-fulfilling tree,

Is supposed to grow on the Earth to help us accomplish all
     our goals.

Long ago, our ancestors ate the fruits of trees

And covered themselves with their leaves.

They learned to make fire by rubbing wood together,

And they took refuge under their branches in case of danger.

Even in this era of science and technology,

Trees provide shelter for us,

Chairs to sit down in and beds to sleep in.

When the heart is burning with the fire of anger, fed by
     arguments,

Trees offer their fresh, welcoming shade.

In trees reside the sighs of all life on Earth.

When they have disappeared,

The continent called by the name of the Jambu tree[23]

Will be nothing but a gloomy, devastated desert.

Nothing is dearer to the living than life.

Having recognized this, in the rules of the Vinaya,

The Buddha establishes prohibitions,

Such as not using water that contains living creatures.

In the remote lands of the Himalayas,

In the old days, in Tibet, they forbade hunting and fishing

And even construction work[24] at certain times.

These traditions are noble, for they preserve and cherish

The lives of the humblest creatures, innocent and defenseless.

Playing with the lives of other beings, without hesitation or
     feeling,

As in sporting activities like hunting or fishing,

Represents senseless and useless violence,

Defying the solemn rights of the living.

While being attentive to the interdependent nature

Of all creatures, both animate and inanimate,

We should never relax our efforts

To protect and preserve the energy of nature.

A special day, in a special month of every year,

Should be dedicated to the planting of a tree.

Thus, we should take up our responsibility toward our brethren,

For our own greatest happiness, and the happiness of all.

May the force of observing what is right,

Abstaining from evil conduct and harmful actions,

Feed the prosperity of the world and increase it!

May such an attitude increase the vigor of living beings

And allow them to flourish!

May pastoral joy and natural happiness

Continue to grow and spread, embracing everything that lives![25]

Our Planet Is *One World*

The Buddha in the Green Party!

IF WE THINK CAREFULLY ABOUT IT, we come to the conclusion that if the Buddha Shakyamuni were to return among us and join a political party, it would be the Green Party! (*Laughs.*) He would be an ecologist! (*Laughs.*)

After all, the Buddha was not born in a paradise, but in a garden.[26] When he became enlightened, it wasn't in an office, a house, or a temple, but in the shade of a tree, the Bodhi Tree.[27] And when he died, it was at the foot of two trees that the Buddha entered great nirvana.[28]

Human rights and the environment

IF I HAD TO vote, it would be for a party that defends the environment. One of the more positive recent developments in the world is the growing realization of the importance of nature. There is nothing sacred or holy about this. As human beings, our life comes from nature, and it is senseless to act against it. That is why I say that the environment is not a question of religion or ethics or morality, all of which are luxuries, since we can do without them and still survive. But we will not survive if we continue to go against nature.

We must accept this reality. If we throw nature off balance, humanity will suffer. Moreover, we who are living today must take into consideration those who will live tomorrow. A clean environment is a human right like any other. So it is our responsibility to hand down a world that is healthy, if not even healthier than we found it. This proposition is not as difficult as it may seem. True, our capacity to act as individuals is limited, but the commitment of everyone is not. Individually, we must do everything we can, no matter how little. Even if turning off the light when you leave a room doesn't seem very consequential, that doesn't mean we shouldn't do it.

On this point, as a Buddhist monk, my feeling is that belief in karma is very useful in everyday life. Once you believe in the connection between the motivation of an action and its effect, you become more sensitive to the repercussions of what you do, for yourself and others. That is the reason why, despite the tragedy that is occurring in Tibet, I find many good things in the world.

I am especially comforted when I see that consumption, taken as an end in itself, seems to be giving way to the feeling that we must preserve the Earth's resources. This is utterly necessary. Human beings are children of the Earth. Whereas our common Mother Earth has tolerated our conduct up to now, she is showing us at present that we have reached the limits of what is tolerable.

I pray I am someday able to pass on this message of protection of the environment and care for others to the people of China. Since Buddhism isn't at all foreign to the Chinese, I think I can be useful to them, on a practical level. The ninth Panchen Lama once gave the Kalachakra initiation in Beijing.[29] So if I were to do the same thing, there would be a precedent. As a Buddhist monk, my concern is for all members of the human family—actually for all sentient beings.

With the growing impact of science on our lives, religion and spirituality have an even larger role to play, by reminding us of our humanity. There is no contradiction between these two approaches. Each one gives us valuable insights that allow us to understand the other better. Both science and the teachings of the Buddha speak to us of the essential unity of all living things.

———————

Many times the Dalai Lama has publicly expressed his desire to confer on his "Chinese brothers and sisters" a Kalachakra initiation in Beijing, on Tiananmen Square. This tantric ritual, regarded as the supreme rite of Tibetan Buddhism, is dedicated to peace in the world.

When he gave the Kalachakra initiation in Sarnath in 1990 after having received the Nobel Peace Prize, the Dalai Lama blessed the seeds of different fruit trees and handed them out to the participants, declaring, "All the continents in the world are represented in this Kalachakra gathering. These seeds were placed near the mandala to receive the blessings. There are apricot, hazelnut, papaya, guava, and other seeds, which can be cultivated at various latitudes."[30] Thus, the world was sown with the seeds of peace.

Mind, heart, and environment

IT IS DIFFICULT for ordinary human beings to understand fully the experts' forecasts on environmental changes. We hear talk of global warming, rising sea levels, increased cancer rates, major demographic growth, the exhaustion of natural resources, and the extinction of species. Everywhere, human activity is causing an accelerated destruction of the key elements on which the natural ecosystem of all living beings rests.

The world population has tripled in the space of a century, and it is expected to be multiplied by two or three in the twenty-first century. With the development of the global economy, extreme increases of energy consumption, production of carbon monoxide, and large-scale deforestation are foreseen. It is hard to imagine—all this will occur during our lifetime and during our children's lifetime. We must anticipate suffering and environmental degradation on a global scale that will surpass anything we've known in the history of humanity.

In my opinion, however, there is still some good news: from now on, we will have to find a way to survive *together* on this planet. We have experienced enough wars, poverty, pollution, and suffering. According to the Buddhist teachings, these tragedies stem from ignorance and selfish actions, because most of the time we can't manage to see the relationship that links all living things together. The Earth is warning us and giving us a clear signal of the large-scale consequences and the negative potential created by misdirected human behavior.

To thwart these harmful practices, let us learn to become more aware of our dependence on one another, and let us engage in correct actions, based on better motivation, to help the Earth and our brethren. That is why I always speak of the importance of an authentic sense of our universal responsibility.

We need knowledge that will allow us to take care of ourselves, of each location on Earth, and of the life it sustains. All this concerns future generations as well, so education on the subject of the environment is a priority for everyone.

Science and technological progress are essential to improve the quality of life in the present world. Even more important is learning to know and appreciate our natural environment more, whether we are adults or children. If we have real concern for others and if we refuse to act inconsiderately, we will be able to take care of the Earth. Let us learn how to share it instead of wanting to own it and destroying the beauty of life.

The ancestral cultures that have adapted to nature show how to create balance between a society and its environment. The Tibetans, as an example, have a unique experience of life on the Himalayan plateau, developed over the long history of a civilization that took care not to overexploit or destroy a fragile ecosystem. We have long appreciated the presence of wild animals, thinking they symbolize freedom. A profound respect for nature is visible in our art and our way of life. Our spiritual development was maintained despite limited material progress. Just as various species cannot adapt to sudden environmental change, human cultures also need to be treated with special consideration to assure their survival. Therefore, studying the ways of life of various peoples and preserving their cultural heritage is one way to learn how to protect the environment.

If we look closely, we see that the human mind, the human heart, and the environment are all inseparable. From this perspective, environmental education allows the birth of both the understanding and the love that we need for a peaceful and lasting coexistence.[31]

Taking care of the Earth

THE EARTH IS NOT only the common heritage of humanity, but also our ultimate source of life. By overexploiting its resources, we are in the process of undermining the very ground of our survival. All around we see the signs of destruction caused by human action and the degradation of nature. So protection and preservation of the Earth are questions not of morality or ethics, but of survival. The way we rise to this challenge will have an impact not just on our generation but on many generations to come.

When it comes to questions that have such a global import, the human mind is the key factor, as is the case in business, international, scientific, technological, medical, or ecological problems. All these seem to go beyond the capacity of individual response, but their root and solution must be sought within the mind. In order to transform the situation outside, we must transform ourselves from within. If you want a beautiful garden, you must first sketch it out in your imagination and have a vision of it. Then the idea can be made concrete, and the external garden will materialize. Destruction of natural resources results from ignorance, from a lack of respect for the living things of the Earth, and from greed.

To begin, we must try to control these negative states of mind by developing an awareness of the interdependent nature of all phenomena, by cultivating a wish not to harm other living beings, and by understanding their need for compassion. Because of the interdependent nature of every living being, we cannot hope to solve a multifaceted question by beginning with partiality or a self-centered attitude. History shows us that peoples haven't often managed to cooperate. Our past failures result from the ignorance of our inter-dependent nature. Today we need a holistic approach to problems linked to an authentic sense of universal responsibility, based on love and compassion.

I offer my best wishes and my prayers so that we can become aware of the necessity to take better care of the Earth.[32]

Interdependence
as seen from space

WHEN WE LOOK AT THE EARTH from space, we don't see any borders, just a little blue planet. *One* planet. The question that arises today is that of the future of the entire planet. It is becoming obvious that our very survival is closely linked to a number of factors. The interdependence taught in Buddhism does not now seem like an ideological abstraction, but like a proven fact, illustrated by this image of the Earth.[33]

———————

The Dalai Lama's position on the subject of ethics, human rights, and the environment introduced to the international scene the notion of interdependence and its corollary, universal responsibility. Thus, since the 1990s, many UN declarations have been written with the aim of inspiring in the peoples of the world a new feeling of interdependence and shared responsibility for the well-being of humanity and all living things.

For example, in the following texts we find the key notions of the Dalai Lama's analysis of the contemporary world: the Charter of Human Responsibilities (December 2002); the Declaration for a Global Ethics, written by the Parliament of the World Religions (Chicago, 1994); the Project for Universal Ethics, developed by UNESCO's Department of Philosophy and Ethics; the Universal Declaration for Human Responsibility (Vienna, 1997); and the Earth Charter, presented at UNESCO (Paris, 2000).

Echoes of the Dalai Lama's analysis can be seen even in the terminology of these documents—as attested, for instance, by this excerpt from the Earth

Charter calling for the creation of a world society at a crucial time in the history of the Earth, a time when humanity must decide its own future:

As the world becomes increasingly interdependent and fragile, the future at once holds great peril and great promise. To move forward we must recognize that in the midst of a magnificent diversity of cultures and life forms we are one human family and one Earth community with a common destiny. We must join together to bring forth a sustainable global society founded on respect for nature, universal human rights, economic justices, and a culture of peace. Towards this end, it is imperative that we, the peoples of the Earth, declare our responsibility to one another, to the greater community of life, and to future generations.

Humanity is part of a vast evolving universe. Earth, our home, is alive with a unique community of life. . . . The global environment with its finite resources is a common concern of all peoples. The protection of the Earth's vitality, diversity, and beauty is a sacred trust. . . .

The choice is ours: form a global partnership to care for Earth and one another or risk the destruction of ourselves and the diversity of life. Fundamental changes are needed in our values, institutions, and ways of living. We must realize that when basic needs have been met, human development is primarily about being more, not having more. . . .

To realize these aspirations, we must decide to live with a sense of universal responsibility, identifying ourselves with the whole Earth community as well as our local communities. . . . Everyone shares responsibility for the present and future well-being of the human family and the larger living world. The spirit of human solidarity and kinship with all life is strengthened when we live with reverence for the mystery of being, gratitude for the gift of life, and humility regarding the human place in nature.

We urgently need a shared vision of basic values to provide an ethical foundation for the emerging world community.[34]

It is interesting to note that the Earth Charter makes a point of defining "the place we occupy as human beings in the universe." If it is necessary to assert our quality as human beings, isn't that a sign that this place is threatened?

Spirituality seems to constitute a final recourse, since it offers a recentering around human values and the meaning of life. It is on this basis that the Dalai Lama has suggested founding a secular ethics for the twenty-first century. He asserts that spirituality allows a revolution of the heart that is capable of awakening our consciousness. The spiritual dimension shows our human potential all that it is capable of by opening up the way for an inner transformation that can lead to transforming the world.

PART THREE

As the Dalai Lama

6

In 1959 the Dalai Lama Meets the World

I Was the Only One Who Could Win Unanimous Support

At sixteen, I become the temporal leader of Tibet

IN OCTOBER 1950, IN their campaigns in eastern Tibet, the People's Liberation Army inflicted heavy losses on our troops, which were greatly inferior in number and poorly equipped. When we learned that the city of Chamdo had fallen into Chinese hands, our fears intensified. Faced with looming danger, the population of Lhasa mobilized to ask that I be made responsible and invested with temporal power.

Announcements were posted on the city's walls, violently criticizing the government and demanding that I immediately take the country's destiny into my own hands. I remember being filled with anxiety when this news reached me. I was only sixteen, and I still had to finish my religious training. What's more, I knew nothing about the upheavals that had occurred in China and that led to the invasion of our country. I had received no political training. So I protested, citing my inexperience and my age, since usually a Dalai Lama relieves a regent of his responsibility at the age of eighteen, not sixteen.

It is clear that the long periods of regency were a weak point of our institutions. I myself had for several years been able to observe the tensions between the various government factions and their deleterious effect on the country's administration. The situation was becoming catastrophic under the threat of Chinese invasion. More than ever, we needed unity, and as the Dalai Lama, I was the only one who could win the country's unanimous support.

My cabinet decided to consult the State Oracle. At the end of the ceremony, the *Kuten,* staggering beneath the weight of his immense ritual headdress, came over to me and placed on my lap a *kata,* the white ceremonial scarf, on which he had written the words *Thu la bap*—"Your time has come."

The oracle had spoken. I had to take on my responsibilities and prepare without delay to lead my country, which was getting ready to enter into war.

———————

On November 17, 1950, the Dalai Lama officially became the temporal leader of Tibet. On October 1, 1949, Mao Tse-tung, victorious over the Nationalists, had proclaimed the birth of the People's Republic of China in Beijing. Beginning in January 1, 1950, he made known his intention to "liberate" Tibet, which the Chinese traditionally called "the House of Western Treasures." In the language of propaganda, "liberation" was a matter of putting an end to "Western imperialism" and to the "reactionary regime" of the last theocracy in the world. At the time, however, there were only seven foreigners in Tibet.

On October 7, 1950, forty thousand men from the People's Liberation Army crossed the Yangtze, the eastern border between Tibet and China. Despite the

*fierce resistance of 8,500 Tibetan soldiers and considerable natural obstacles,
the advance of the Chinese troops was relentless. It stopped only a hundred
kilometers away from the capital, Lhasa.*

*The Tibetan government was summoned to send a delegation to Bei-
jing to negotiate with the Chinese authorities the conditions of "peaceful
liberation."*

We wrongly believed that isolation would guarantee us peace

THE THREAT TO THE FREEDOM of Tibet had not escaped the world's notice. The Indian government, supported by the British, protested to the authorities of the People's Republic of China in November 1950, declaring that the invasion of our territory threatened peace. But it was all in vain. We would have to pay the price of our ancestral isolation.

Geography cut our territory off from the rest of the world. Before, in Tibet, in order to reach the borders of India and Nepal, one had to plan for a long, difficult, monthlong journey from Lhasa through high Himalayan passes that were uncrossable for most of the year.

Isolation, then, is a characteristic feature of our country, and we had deliberately reinforced it by authorizing the presence of only a small number of foreigners. In the past, Lhasa was even called "the Forbidden City." It is true that historically our relations with the neighboring peoples—Mongols, Manchus, and Chinese—were antagonistic. Above all, though, we wanted to live in peace, in the spirit of our religion. We had thought we could continue this peaceful way of life by remaining apart from the world. This was a mistake. And today I make it a duty to leave my door wide open to everyone.

The Dalai Lama rightly regrets that, out of a lack of interest in foreign politics and a lack of experience in international relations, Tibet neglected to make its independence officially known to the community of nations. The occasion had presented itself to the Thirteenth Dalai Lama, who, during the first Chinese revolution in 1911, had proclaimed his country's independence and expelled from Lhasa the Manchu ambans (the representatives of the emperor), along with a small garrison of Chinese soldiers.

In the beginning of the twentieth century, Tibet fulfilled all the criteria for de facto state sovereignty. It possessed a territory with defined borders and a government exercising its plenary authority and maintaining international relations. In 1947, during the Asian Relations Conference in New Delhi, the Tibetan delegates sat, along with their flag, among the representatives of thirty-two nations. But Tibetan diplomacy was limited to contacts with bordering countries: British and then, in 1947, independent India, Nepal, Bhutan, and China. This status of de facto independence was not legalized through international recognition.

The independence of Tibet in relation to China lends itself to contradictory interpretations because of the complex and often misunderstood relations between the two countries, in each of which politics and religion have long been entangled. After having been in the past a warring kingdom that fought in Mongolia, China, and the city-states on the Silk Road, Tibet comprised, at its military apogee in the eighth century, Indo-European peoples, Turks, and Chinese, and even occupied the Chinese capital of Chang'an. Though conquered by the Mongols in the tenth century, Tibet was never integrated into their empire.

A spiritual master–lay protector relationship was established between the Tibetan Dalai Lamas and the Khans of Mongolia,[1] and when, in the thirteenth century, the Mongols established the Yuan dynasty in China, the same link was established between the Son of Heaven and the Dalai Lama. The emperor of China was regarded by the Tibetans as an earthly emanation of Manjushri, the bodhisattva of enlightened Wisdom, and a power of temporal protection was assigned to him. The Dalai Lama, whose reincarnation lineage descends from Avalokiteshvara, the bodhisattva of enlightened

Compassion, exercised a spiritual authority that was respected in both China and Mongolia.

In the context of this special relationship, in the eighteenth century the Chinese army intervened to reestablish the Seventh Dalai Lama on his throne when Tibet was torn apart by a civil war. Two ambans settled in Lhasa, but they were required to report to the Dalai Lama's government, and they never exercised any prerogative on behalf of China.

Later on, in the twentieth century, Tibet became a stake in Central Asia when it aroused the greed of both Russia and the United Kingdom. First the British tried to sign commercial agreements with China about Tibet and to redraw unilaterally the borders of the Himalayan kingdoms. But the Tibetans protested the validity of these treaties.

In 1904 a British military expedition tried to impose the supremacy of Great Britain by force, and the Thirteenth Dalai Lama had to flee his occupied capital. The English and the regent signed the Convention of Lhasa, which designated war compensation and bestowed commercial advantages on the British. This treaty established a de facto recognition of Tibetan sovereignty in relation to the Chinese nation. It was confirmed in 1906 by the document that the British signed with the Chinese, which explicitly accepted the Anglo-Tibetan treaty.

Still, in 1907, to confirm their advantages, the British renegotiated with the Chinese and concluded the Treaty of Peking, in which they agreed not to deal with Tibet except through the intermediary of China. In flagrant contradiction to the previous agreements, this new treaty explicitly recognized a Chinese "suzerainty" over Tibet. Thus, a historic countertruth was legitimized, forming the basis for later Chinese claims that Tibet was part of China.

The Dalai Lama deplored the contradictions in the Treaty of Peking, the consequences of which would turn out to be grave for his country: "Suzerainty is a vague and ancient term. Perhaps it was the nearest western *political term to describe the relations between Tibet and China from 1720 to 1890, but still, it was very inaccurate, and the use of it has misled whole generations of western statesmen. It did not take into account the reciprocal spiritual relationship, or recognize that the relationship was a personal matter between the Dalai Lamas and the Manchu emperors. There are many such ancient eastern relationships which cannot be described in ready-made western political terms."[2] Subsequent Tibetan protests before the United Nations did not succeed in overriding Chinese authority and having Tibetan sovereignty accepted.*

I endorse the Kashag's appeal
to the United Nations

O N NOVEMBER 7, 1950, the Kashag [the Tibetan cabinet] and the government appealed to the United Nations, asking them to intercede for us. I approved of the terms of the letter:

> The attention of the world is riveted on Korea where aggression is being resisted by an international force. Similar happenings in remote Tibet are passing without notice. It is in the belief that aggression will not go unchecked and freedom unprotected in any part of the world that we have assumed the responsibility of reporting to the United Nations Organization, through you, recent happenings in the border area of Tibet.
>
> As you are aware, the problem of Tibet has taken on proportions in recent times. This problem is not of Tibet's own making but is largely the outcome of unthwarted Chinese ambition to bring weaker nations on its periphery under its active domination.[3]

The strategy of the People's Republic of China was to make the Western world believe that it was sincerely committed to a peaceful settlement of the Tibetan question. The leading nations were at the time preoccupied by the threat of nuclear war, with Korea at the epicenter of that concern, and the Soviet Union had declared its support for Maoist China. The only UN member country to launch an appeal against the invasion of foreign forces into

Tibet was El Salvador, in November 1950. Prime Minister Jawaharlal Nehru of India, who was concerned about preserving his friendship with his great neighbor in the north, refused to intervene. Great Britain showed itself indifferent, and the United States took the side of prudence for fear of aggravating its relations with the Soviets.

On Tibetan soil, however, the Chinese armies were perpetrating acts of violence in eastern Tibet. The Tibetan government had sent a delegation to Beijing to negotiate. But the discussions came to an abrupt halt, and threatened with a forced march on Lhasa, on May 23, 1951, the Tibetan emissaries signed the Agreement for Peaceful Liberation of Tibet, also called the Seventeen-Point Agreement, which organized the annexation of their country by China.

According to the International Commission of Jurists,[4] this text is worthless under international law because it was signed under the threat of weapons.

The motherland, a shameless lie

I USED TO LISTEN TO the broadcasts of Radio Beijing in Tibetan. One night when I was alone, I suddenly heard a shrill voice announcing that the Seventeen-Point Agreement for the Peaceful Liberation of Tibet had just been signed between representatives of the government of the People's Republic of China and the so-called regional government of Tibet.

I couldn't believe my ears. I wanted to jump up and call out to everyone, but I was riveted to my seat. The announcer explained that "during the last century, aggressive imperialist forces had invaded Tibet to perpetrate all sorts of abuses and provocations there. The result of this," he said, "was that the Tibetan people were plunged into the profound sufferings of slavery." I felt physically ill when I heard this improbable mixture of lies and the clichés of fantastic propaganda.

But the worst was yet to come. The radio announced that, according to the first clause of the agreement, the Tibetan people would be returned to their "motherland." That Tibet could return to the motherland was a shameless lie! Tibet was never part of China. On the contrary, it could even claim large Chinese territories. Our peoples are ethnically different, and radically so. We don't speak the same language, and our writing has nothing in common with Chinese characters.

The most alarming thing was that the Tibetan delegates were not authorized to sign in my name. Their sole mission was to negotiate; I had kept the state seals with me.

The Dalai Lama was confronted with a dilemma. In his entourage, his older brother, Takster Rinpoche, had fled the Kumbum monastery and made contact with foreign diplomatic missions in Calcutta. He was convinced that the Americans would not tolerate the Communist expansionism of the Chinese and that they would fight for Tibet. Knowing that the United States was already militarily engaged in Korea, the Dalai Lama doubted that it would open a second front in Tibet. What's more, realizing that China was a much more populated country, he feared that an armed conflict, even if supported by a foreign power, would be extremely long and bloody. To try to avoid bloodshed with an uncertain outcome, the young Dalai Lama decided to meet the Chinese leaders. Thinking that they were human beings too, he hoped to be able to discuss things with them and reach an agreement.

Mao's personality impressed me

DESPITE THE CONTEXT of difficult relations with China, in 1954 and 1955 I went to that country. It was a good chance to discover a different world. What's more, during this trip I met many Tibetans in the provinces of Kham and Amdo, so I acquired a number of new experiences and acquaintances. I also met many leaders, notably President Mao Tse-tung. I first saw him during a public meeting. When I entered the room where he was, I noticed first a battery of spotlights. Mao in person was sitting in their light, very calm and relaxed. He didn't look like a particularly intelligent man. When I shook his hand, though, I felt as if I were in the presence of a great magnetic force. He behaved in a very friendly, spontaneous way, despite protocol.

All in all, I had at least a dozen meetings with him, most of them during large gatherings, but a few in private. On these occasions, whether they were banquets or conferences, he always had me sit next to him, and once he even served me food.

I found him very impressive. Physically, he was very unusual. He had a dark complexion, but his skin seemed to gleam, as if he were wearing skin cream. His hands were very beautiful and had that same strange glow, with perfect fingers and exquisitely shaped thumbs. I noticed that he seemed to have difficulty breathing, and he wheezed a lot. Perhaps that affected his way of speaking, which was always very slow and precise. He seemed partial to short sentences, probably for the same reason. His movements and gestures were also very slow. It took him several seconds to move his head from left to right, which gave him a dignified, self-assured air.

Our final interview took place in the spring of 1955, the day before my departure, in his office. I had visited several Chinese provinces by then and I was getting ready to say to him in all sincerity that I was strongly interested in different development projects for Tibet. But he came over to me and murmured, "Your behavior is correct because you are learned. But believe me, religion is a poison that has two serious defects: it reduces the population, since monks and nuns take the vow of celibacy, and it curbs progress. It has produced two victims, Tibet and Mongolia."

At these words, I was filled with a burning sensation in my face and an intense fear.

The Dalai Lama left China without illusions. But he candidly observed that people in trouble always tend to cling to the slightest hope, so he tried again to find common ground with the occupier, whose presence had been reinforced in his absence.

After the signing of the Seventeen-Point Agreement, the People's Liberation Army had continued its advance, occupying Lhasa and central Tibet, in violation of the official guarantees that had been given. The Chinese Communist Party went on to demolish the eastern Tibetan provinces, which passed under the administration of different regions in the People's Republic, since Mao decided, in 1955, to include them in "the great tide of socialist transformation."

Between 1950 and 1959, the upkeep of the occupation troops and the first land collectives sparked a famine, while forced labor was instituted to build strategic roads. When, starting from the "Great Leap Forward" of 1958, the democratic reforms entailed the forced denunciation of Tibetan leaders and respected lamas, popular revolt spread. The Chinese authorities reinforced the occupying force with additional troops as armed resistance against the occupier became more radical in the eastern reaches of Tibet in Kham and Amdo.

March 10, 1959, a day of insurrection in Lhasa

AFTER MY PRAYERS AND BREAKFAST [on March 10, 1959], I went out into the light of a calm morning and strolled through the garden. The sky was crystal-clear, and the sun rays lit up the top of the mountain that overlooked Drepung monastery in the distance. Soon they were shining on the palace and shrines and on Norbulingka, the Jewel Park, where I was walking. It was a fresh, cheerful spring, with tufts of new grass and fragile buds opening on the poplar and willow trees. Lotus leaves were poking up through the surface of the pool and spreading in the sun. Suddenly I jumped when I heard shouts in the distance.

I sent some guards to find out the reason for these cries. When they returned, they explained to me that the population was streaming out of Lhasa toward Norbulingka in large numbers, to protect me from the Chinese. They kept pouring out all morning. Some remained grouped together at the different entrances to the park, while others were starting to patrol around it. By noon about thirty thousand people had gathered there. The situation had to be defused.

I was afraid that, in a burst of rage, the crowd might try to fight with the Chinese garrison. Spontaneously elected leaders called to the Chinese to give Tibet back to the Tibetans. Everyone demanded the end of the occupation and the reestablishment of the Dalai Lama's authority. Hearing their shouts, I realized the fury of the demonstrators, and I knew that they had become uncontrollable.

I felt caught between two volcanoes. On one side, my people were rebelling as one against the Chinese regime. On the other, a powerful and aggressive occupation force was standing, ready to charge. If a battle broke out, the inhabitants of Lhasa would be massacred by the thousands and the rest of the country would be subjected to an implacable martial law, with its inevitable crimes and persecutions.

———————————

On March 10, 1959, when the Chinese army, stationed around Lhasa, aimed its cannons at the Dalai Lama's summer residence, thousands of Tibetans spontaneously gathered to form a wall with their bodies. The crowd did not disperse in the days that followed, and when, on March 17, the Chinese army attacked, men, women, old people, and children offered their lives for the Dalai Lama.

In street battles that set twenty thousand Tibetans against forty thousand Chinese soldiers, the Lhasa insurrection of 1959 continued for three days and three nights before it was repressed. In Lhasa, devastated by mortar fire and submachine guns, the survivors say that the corpses of men, dogs, and horses barred the narrow streets flowing with blood. On the morning of March 18, 1959, dawn rose on the death rattles of the dying, the groans of the wounded, and the stench of widespread blood.

There were about ten thousand dead, and four thousand demonstrators were arrested. Arrests and summary executions continued for a long time after the events.

The day before the massacre, disguised as a soldier, the Dalai Lama had fled. Under the protection of the Freedom Fighters—resisters who came from Kham—he had taken the road of exile to India, hoping that his departure could spare the massacre of his followers. But his wish was not granted.

My Children, You Are
the Future of Tibet

Forced exile

WE MUST HAVE BEEN a sorry sight when we were welcomed by the Indian border guards. There were eighty of us, all physically exhausted by the journey and morally overwhelmed by the ordeal.

When we arrived in Tezpur,⁵ hundreds of messages, letters, and telegrams were waiting for me. People from all over the world sent me their greetings and encouragements. I was overwhelmed with gratitude, but also with a sense of urgency. The priority was to prepare a brief declaration for the many people who were waiting for a word from me to relay to the media. So I reported the facts frankly and in moderate terms. Then, after a light lunch, we took the train for Mussoorie.

Hundreds or even thousands of people rushed to see us as we traveled by, waving at us and wishing us welcome. In some places they even had to clear the tracks so we could move forward. The news spread quickly throughout the Indian countryside, and it seemed as if everyone knew about my presence on board that train. Thousands came one after the other to welcome me with shouts of "Dalai Lama Ki Jai! Dalai Lama Zindabad!" (Long live the Dalai Lama! Long life to the Dalai Lama!).

I was very moved. In three large cities on my journey—Siliguri, Benares, and Lucknow—I had to leave the train car and take part in impromptu meetings with immense crowds that welcomed me by tossing flowers. The whole journey seemed like an extraordinary dream. When I think back on it, I am infinitely grateful to the people of India for their effusive kindness at that moment of my life.

A few days later a communiqué from the Chinese news agency arrived, condemning my Tezpur statement as "a gross document full of faulty reasoning, lies, and subterfuge." According to the Chinese version of events, I had been kidnapped by Lhasa rebels acting in the pay of "imperialist aggressors."

I was stunned to find that the Chinese were accusing imaginary imperialists, such as the Tibetans residing in India, the Indian government, and my "clique in power," instead of admitting the truth that the people they were claiming to liberate had revolted against them.

In 1959 the Dalai Lama met the world and the world met Tibet. But the international press dwelled mostly on the exotic nature of Tibetan culture, with articles that foregrounded a mixture of the fantastic and the religious, and relegated the political question of China's illegal occupation of Tibet to the background. Thus, Paris Match, in its April 28, 1959, issue, glorified "the Tibetan Joan of Arc" who was supposed to have miraculously guided the Dalai Lama during his journey through the highest mountain passes in the world. The magazine didn't shrink from praising the supernatural powers of the young spiritual master, whom it compared to a magician summoning the protection of benevolent spirits he knew how to tame.

The situation, however, was only getting worse in Tibet. Learning that the Dalai Lama had managed to reach India, Mao is said to have cried out, "We have lost the war!" But the pace of so-called democratic reforms only accelerated in all the regions of Tibet, none of which were spared. The Chinese Communist Party completely eliminated the Tibetan ruling class; all opponents were massacred, lamas were arrested, and the religious and artistic treasures of monasteries were looted. In central Tibet, out of 2,500 monasteries, only 70 were spared.

The Chinese occupation caused tens of thousands of deaths in a few years; multiple testimonials gave the same reports: Tibetans were not only sent to the firing squad but burned alive, drowned, strangled, hanged, buried alive, drawn and quartered, and decapitated.

Between March 1959 and 1960, eighty thousand Tibetans followed the Dalai Lama on the roads to exile. Nehru's support needed to be won if the lives of the Tibetans who had taken refuge in India were to be organized into a functioning community. Nehru, however, although sincerely desirous of aiding the Tibetans, was anxious to maintain good relations with Maoist China.

My priority is stopping
the bloodshed

O N APRIL 24, 1959, Pandit Jawaharlal Nehru came to see me in person in Mussoorie.[6] Our interview lasted for several hours, in the presence of a single interpreter. I undertook to tell him in detail what had happened since I had returned from Beijing to Tibet, following his insistent advice.[7] I went on to declare that I had acted toward the Chinese as he had suggested, with justice and honesty, criticizing them when there was reason to do so, while still trying to preserve the terms of the Seventeen-Point Agreement.

At certain points in our conversation, Nehru hit the table with his fist. "How is that possible?" he exclaimed once or twice. I continued, even though it was obvious that he could be a little abrupt. To conclude, I told him very firmly that my main concern was twofold: "I am determined to regain Tibet's independence, but for now, my priority is to put an end to the bloodbath." At these words, Nehru couldn't restrain himself anymore. "That's not possible," he said in a voice full of emotion. "You say that you want independence and at the same time that you don't want a bloodbath. Impossible!" His lower lip was trembling with rage as he spoke.

I began to realize that the prime minister found himself in an extremely delicate and embarrassing position. In the Indian Parliament, a tense new debate on the Tibetan question had followed the news of my escape. For years Nehru had been criticized by many politicians on his position toward me. I understood that my future and the future of my people were much less certain than I had imagined.

Nehru's reserved political support was accompanied by an exemplary commitment to organizing the education of Tibetan children. Many Tibetan children had arrived in India with their families, who had lost everything, and Nehru, aware of their tragedy, suggested to the Dalai Lama that specialized schools be made for them so as to preserve the Tibetan language and culture. An independent organization for the education of Tibetans, within the Indian Ministry of Education, was set up, and school buildings were constructed at government expense.

Children of hope

NOT LONG AFTER our tumultuous arrival in India, I offered the following words of encouragement to my new exiled community.

"My children, we want to make you all into devoted, useful members of our community. You should work with all your heart for the people, the religion, and the cause of Tibet.

"My children, you are human beings. You are neither plants nor flowers, which fade in the heat of the sun or are destroyed and scattered by hail and storms. Unlike plants, you can take your fate in hand. Whatever physical sufferings you may endure, you should always keep a clear conscience and a stable, solid mind.

"The Red Chinese have caused each of us great suffering. We should not forget these atrocities. You should work hard to acquire knowledge and fight with the weapons of justice and law. Day and night, you should strive to acquire greater culture in order to serve your religion and your people. That is your personal responsibility.

"My children, you should continue the work begun by your elders. Let's not stand aside and do nothing, as if we were waiting for rain to fall from the sky. We all have to work hard. Young and old, let us try to realize our common objective.

"My children, the more I look at you, the happier I feel. You represent the hope for a better tomorrow, and you will manage to overcome the difficulties that lie ahead. You are at the threshold of existence; you should become stronger each day, without wasting your precious time. You are the future of Tibet."[8]

In April 1960, one year after exile began, the spokesman for a camp in Jammu came to see His Holiness with alarming news. During the transfer of a group of refugees to Ladakh, a blizzard had blown up. With exposure to the cold added to malnutrition and lack of medical care, the children had been decimated.

The fate of children was an absolute priority for the Dalai Lama. In Tibet the Chinese had begun a campaign of "patriotic reeducation," separating children from their parents and even deporting the smartest ones to China. As for the young refugees in India, they were threatened by hunger and disease. An entire generation was in danger.

The Dalai Lama's decision was immediate. He asked members of his family and officials in his entourage to take charge of the sick or malnourished children by creating a building for the purpose with the help of the Indian government. An emissary was sent to the refugees with the following message:

"Your life is very hard. I have decided to create an establishment that will welcome your children. If you entrust them to me, that will simplify your life and your children will learn to be independent and to count on themselves.

"What's more, they will become real Tibetans, heirs of our newfound freedom. They will never forget their parents, their ancestors, their brothers and sisters, their compatriots who sacrificed themselves for them. Of course, I am not imposing this by force; parents and children can make their own choice freely."

When the spokesman had finished, there was a moment of silence. Then the father of a little four-year-old girl spoke. He had not accepted the indoctrination that prevented Tibetans from being Tibetan in their own country and forced them to condemn their people, their homeland, and their religion. So with his daughter perched on his shoulders, he and his wife had followed the Dalai Lama's footsteps beyond the Himalayas. "I think," he concluded, "that an excellent chance is given us in offering to care for and educate our children."

The disabled grandmother of a little Tibetan boy stood up to say, "I have prayed to see with my own eyes the death of those who committed such atrocities in our country. Unfortunately, I am too old; I think I will die here. But there is my grandson and all the other children. So I pray that they can be taken care of so they can prepare to avenge all our dead soon."

The father of another child also declared, "I pray I see Tibet free as before, before I die. Long live the Dalai Lama!" The refugees repeated, "Long live the Dalai Lama!" And the children themselves asked their parents to let them go to the Dalai Lama, to the establishment he had created for them.

In 1960, at the same time that the Dalai Lama's immediate entourage was taking responsibility for the children, the Indian government opened secondary schools under the authority of an autonomous administration. That same year a Tibetan minister of the interior, in collaboration with Indian and international authorities, was charged with overseeing the assimilation of refugees, who were spread all over India in about fifty camps.

The Dalai Lama also organized a Ministry of Culture and Religion to rebuild all the great monasteries and their universities in the land of exile.

Already during his brief reign, in Tibet itself, the Dalai Lama had undertaken the modernization of Tibetan feudal society. In exile, he introduced democracy to his government by adopting in 1961 a temporary constitution that established a distribution of authority, equality of citizens before the law, free elections, and political pluralism.[9]

This democratization, along with the beginning of the secularization of Tibetan political institutions, was the Dalai Lama's best response to Chinese propaganda that accused him of wanting to restore his personal power.

I am a proponent of
secular democracy

EVEN THOUGH NO BUDDHIST SOCIETY has ever developed a democratic system in its government, I personally have great admiration for secular democracy. When Tibet was still free, we cultivated the isolation that nature had given us, wrongly thinking that we could guarantee our internal peace and security that way. Paying no attention to the changes the world was going through, we almost didn't notice that India, one of our closest neighbors, had become the largest democracy in the world after peacefully winning independence. Later on, we had to suffer to learn that, on the international scene as at home, freedom must be shared and is enjoyed in the company of others. One cannot make exclusive use of freedom.

Although the Tibetans outside of Tibet have been reduced to the status of refugees, we have the freedom to exercise our rights. Our brothers and sisters in Tibet do not have the same right to live in their own country. That is why we exiles have the responsibility of anticipating and imagining the Tibet of the future. Over the years we have put into play a model of authentic democracy in various ways. The fact that the word *democracy* is familiar to all exiled Tibetans attests to this.

I have long awaited the time when we could define a political system that was adapted both to our traditions and to the demands of the modern world, a democracy rooted in nonviolence and peace. We recently instituted some changes that will reinforce the democratization of our administration in exile. For several reasons, I decided that I will not be the leader, or even a part of the government, the day Tibet regains its independence. The next leader of the Tibetan government should be elected by popular vote. There are many advantages to such a reform, which will allow us to become an authentic, complete democracy. I hope that, thanks to these changes, our people will be able to express themselves clearly on decisions that concern the future of Tibet.

Our process of democratization has touched Tibetans all over the world. I think that future generations will look at these transformations as the main accomplishments of our experience in exile. Just as the introduction of Buddhism to Tibet forged our nation, I am convinced that the democratization of our society will reinforce the vitality of Tibetans and allow our governing institutions to reflect their dearest desires and aspirations.[10]

Liberty, equality, and fraternity
are also Buddhist principles

THE IDEA THAT PEOPLE can live freely as individuals who are equal in principle and hence responsible for one another is perfectly in keeping with Buddhism. As Buddhists, we Tibetans respect human life as the most precious gift, believing that the Buddha's philosophy and teaching is the way to the highest of freedoms—an aim that can be reached by men and women alike.

The Buddha saw that the aim of life is happiness. He also saw that, while ignorance leads beings into endless frustration and suffering, wisdom frees them. Modern democracy is based on the principle that all human beings are equal, that each of us has the right to live freely and happily. Buddhism also recognizes that human beings have a right to dignity, that all members of the human family have an equal and inalienable right to be free. This freedom is expressed not just on the political level but also on the basic level, where everyone should be free from fear and need. Whether rich or poor, educated or not, whatever country we come from, whatever religion we follow, whatever ideology we espouse, each of us is above all a human being like any other. Not only do we all want happiness and try to avoid suffering, but it is legitimate to pursue these aims.

The institution established by the Buddha is the *Sangha*, or monastic community, which itself observes democratic rules. In such a fraternity, individuals are equal, regardless of social class or native caste. The only subtle distinction rests on seniority in ordination.

Individual freedom, on the model of Liberation or Enlightenment, was the main goal of the entire community, and it was accomplished by cultivating the mind in meditation. Everyday relationships were based on generosity, respect, and attention to others. By leading a life without a fixed abode, monks detached themselves from possessiveness, without living in total isolation. The custom of begging only reinforced the awareness of their dependence. Within the community, decisions were made by vote, and disagreements settled by consensus. Thus, the Sangha was exemplary in terms of social equality, sharing of resources, and democratic process.[11]

During his trip to China in 1954, the Dalai Lama declared his enthusiasm for Marxism, allowing that the socialist economy is closer to the Buddhist ideal than ruthless capitalism. In Marx's philosophy he found the principles of equality and social justice dear to Buddhism: "My mind could well be redder than the Chinese leaders. In China the Communist regime is governing without Communist ideals," he declared again in 2008, in expressing his dream of a synthesis between Buddhism and Marxism that could turn out to be highly effective in politics.[12]

I love the image of swords
transformed into plowshares

On October 17, 2007, in the rotunda of the U.S. Capitol Building in Washington, it was again in his capacity as a human being that the Dalai Lama received the Congressional Gold Medal, almost twenty years after receiving the Nobel Peace Prize in Oslo.

He mounted the podium in traditional monastic dress: a large saffron shawl was draped over his burgundy robes, leaving his right shoulder free. Around him, solemn statues fixed in marble the memory of the heroic time of Thomas Jefferson and the founding fathers of the American nation, and frescoes commemorated the battles in which George Washington, Lafayette, and other patriots fought for the independence of the United States.

President George W. Bush moved the audience when he mentioned that as a little boy the Dalai Lama "kept a model of the Statue of Liberty at his bedside. Years later, on his first visit to America, he went to Battery Park in New York City so he could see the real thing up close."

The president continued on the theme of liberty, recalling that his forefathers won their independence through a revolution and that "Jefferson counted freedom of worship as one of America's greatest blessings." According to the president, "This freedom does not belong to one nation, it belongs to the world."

The president spoke on behalf of the American government. To defend freedom, his country has resorted to force. Speaking as policeman of the world and as the head of the most militarily powerful nation, George W. Bush defended a peace threatened by terrorism.

The Dalai Lama, however, spoke as a human being and advocated a path of peace toward peace.

––––––––––––

There is a magnificent passage in the Bible that urges us to transform swords into plowshares. I love this image of a weapon made into a tool in the service of basic human needs. It symbolizes an attitude of inner and outer disarmament. In the spirit of this ancient message, it seems important to me today to emphasize the urgency of a policy that is long overdue: to demilitarize the entire planet.[13]

––––––––––––

Peace is not decreed, nor is it imposed by force. The fruit of compassion, peace "ripens in the human heart and shines on the world," the Dalai Lama tells us.

Human beings prefer
the way of peace

I AM SURE THAT EVERYONE AGREES on the necessity for overcoming violence, but in order to eliminate it completely, it must first be analyzed.

From a strictly practical standpoint, we note that violence can sometimes be useful. A problem is resolved more quickly by force. But such a success is often obtained at the expense of the rights and well-being of others. Any problem resolved that way engenders yet another problem.

If solid reasoning is put to the service of a cause, violence is useless. When one is motivated solely by a selfish wish and cannot get what one wants through logic, one resorts to force. Even in the framework of a simple family argument or friendly disagreement, if you support yourself with valid reasoning, you will tirelessly defend your position, point by point. If you lack reasonable motives, however, you are soon overcome with anger, which is never a sign of strength, but of weakness.

In the end, it is important to examine one's motivations, as well as those of the adversary. Violence and nonviolence can take many forms, which are hard to distinguish if one keeps solely to an external viewpoint. A negative motivation produces a profoundly violent action, even when it seems friendly and gentle. On the other hand, a sincere, positive motivation is essentially nonviolent in practice, even if circumstances impose a certain severity. In any case, I have the feeling that only compassionate concern for others can justify recourse to force.

I have heard some Westerners say that in the long run the nonviolent methods of passive resistance advocated by Gandhi are not suitable for everyone and that they are more appropriate in the East. Being more active, Westerners expect immediate results, whatever the situation, even at the cost of their lives. I think this attitude is not always the best one. On the contrary, the practice of nonviolence is beneficial in every case. It simply requires determination. Even though the liberation movements in Eastern Europe quickly attained their goal, nonviolent protest, by its very nature, usually requires patience.

With this in mind, I pray that the supporters of a democratic movement in China remain peaceful, despite the brutality of repression and the difficulties that lie ahead for them. I am sure they will remain peaceful. The majority of young Chinese who are members of it were all born and grew up in a very harsh Communist regime. But in the spring of 1989, they spontaneously put into practice the strategy of passive resistance dear to Mahatma Gandhi. I see in this a clear indication that, as a last resort, human beings prefer the way of peace, despite all indications to the contrary.

Gandhi is the political model for nonviolent struggle, and his portrait is present in many Tibetan administrative offices. A great figure of peace and reconciliation, the Mahatma was honored posthumously at the same time as the Dalai Lama during the awarding of the Nobel Peace Prize. By doing so, the Nobel Committee meant to repair its mistake in not having conferred this distinction on him before.

To win India's independence from British colonial power, Gandhi organized not just nonviolent resistance but also civil disobedience, noncooperation with the occupiers, and protest marches. When the Dalai Lama is reproached for limiting Gandhi's inheritance to nonviolence, he points out that the context does not allow them to reproduce in Tibet the methods that freed India from English control. Gandhi could in fact defend himself freely in a court of law, and although the colonial regime of the British Raj was severe, it still respected the basic rights of individuals, which is not the case with the Chinese authorities. Therefore, the Dalai Lama advocates cultivating the spirit of Gandhi's struggle while adapting it to the Tibetan situation.

What would Gandhi have
done in my place?

MY FIRST VISIT to New Delhi was to the Rajghat, Mahatma Gandhi's cremation site. I wondered what shrewd advice he would have given me if he had still been alive. I thought he would certainly have put all his strength, all his willpower, and his whole personality into a nonviolent campaign for the freedom of the Tibetan people. That comforted me in my decision always to follow his example, whatever obstacles may arise. And more than ever, I resolved not to associate myself with any act of violence.

———————

The Dalai Lama never wavered from his initial decision to respond to Chinese aggression with nonviolence. Ever since the start of his country's occupation, he has tried to open up a dialogue with Beijing and defend the rights of Tibet in the context of the Seventeen-Point Agreement, despite its blatant unfairness. When, in 1958, the armed rebellion of the Khampas became more radical in the east of the country, he asked them to surrender their weapons. These Freedom Fighters had vowed to fight to the death for Tibet. Since they could neither break this vow nor disobey the Dalai Lama, many of them took their own lives.

To this day, the spiritual leader of the Tibetans has persisted in the path of nonviolence. During the Lhasa riots of 1987 and 1988, he was happy to see monks who had gotten hold of Chinese rifles breaking them instead of turning them against the occupier, thus saying no to the language of weapons.

In March 2008, when the inhabitants of Lhasa rose up and committed anti-Chinese acts of violence, the Beijing government accused the Dalai Lama of instigating these actions. The Dalai Lama replied that in that case they would have to take the Nobel Peace Prize away from him, and he challenged the Chinese authorities to come to Dharamsala to investigate and try to prove their allegations.

But he deplored the fact that at the same time as the monks were engaged in peaceful protests, which were cruelly repressed, some young Tibetans were organizing lootings, fires, and robberies. While admitting that their actions had been inspired by despair and by having been treated as second-class citizens in their own country, he condemned the use of violence and declared that if his people strayed from the nonviolent path, he could no longer be their spokesman.

Commenting on the choice of nonviolence from a political standpoint, Samdhong Rinpoche asserts that this method has produced unhoped-for results in terms of international sympathy for the Tibetan cause. If armed combat had been encouraged by the Dalai Lama, it would not have met with success, and by now Tibet would have sunk into oblivion.[14]

7

I Appeal to All the Peoples of the World

I Denounce the Sinicization of Tibet

I ask the world not to forget that thousands of Tibetans were massacred

ON MARCH 10, 1959, the Tibetan people proclaimed the independence of Tibet, after having suffered almost nine years of occupation. A foreign government is, unfortunately, still present in Tibet, but I am proud that the spirit of our people is not crushed and remains unwavering in its resolution to fight until we regain our independence. I know that the struggle that was begun some years ago against the occupier is still going on in Tibet against the invader and oppressor, who hides under the name and appearance of a "liberator." I can confidently declare that the civilized world is learning more every day how those who claim they act in the name of liberty are crushing the liberty of their defenseless neighbors.

The world has become aware of the terrible events that occurred in Tibet thanks to two enlightening reports by the International Commission of Jurists. These documents pointed out that the Chinese wildly flouted the basic human rights of our people, who had been massacred by the thousands solely because they wanted to assert their freedom to live in keeping with their cultural and religious heritage. The documents also emphasized that the Chinese made themselves guilty of genocide for having killed many Tibetans with the intention of destroying the Tibetan religion and for having deported thousands of children to China.

The sympathy these events aroused throughout the world was shown by the United Nations resolution in 1959 calling for the end of the exactions that are depriving the Tibetan people of their basic human rights and historic autonomy. I assert that we have been dispossessed, not of autonomy, but of independence. As for the Chinese, this appeal fell on deaf ears. Things have only gotten worse, as shown by the continuous, incessant flood of refugees coming from Tibet.

The question was discussed in plenary session at the United Nations assembly. I appealed to all those who support us and to the assembly itself that China [be urged to] put an end to its aggression by restoring Tibet's independence. Half-measures would not be much help. Our gratitude went out to the federation of countries that have supported our cause—Malaysia, Thailand, and El Salvador. I appealed to India, our powerful neighbor that continues to welcome thousands of Tibetan refugees, to use its influence to support our cause.

I am aware that Tibetans in Tibet are bearing the torments brought about by foreign domination. I appeal to them to keep their courage and their resolve to regain their independence intact. For my part, I should point out that I am far from pleased to be so far from my country and my beloved and courageous people. I want to tell them that I share their hope and their pain.

To my thousands of compatriots in India, Nepal, Bhutan, and Sikkim, I want to say that we all bear the heavy responsibility of preparing ourselves for the day we can return home and build an independent, happier, greater Tibet. The new Tibet will need thousands of learned, skillful men and women, capable of democratizing it without betraying our cultural and religious heritage or denying our soul.

During the Chinese occupation, before I had to leave Tibet, the Kashag and I tried to introduce land reforms and other changes to Tibet, but as everyone knows, our efforts were cut short by the Chinese. The Communists are today imposing so-called reforms that have a stranglehold on our people. I have studied them carefully and have come to the conclusion that, as they are applied, the Tibetan people will be reduced to a mental and economic state of servitude.

Such reforms conform neither to the United Nations Charter nor to the Universal Declaration of Human Rights. The reforms I envisage should introduce a fair distribution of the country's wealth while preserving intellectual, moral, and religious freedom. On this subject, I will repeat what I declared some time ago now in Dalhousie: "To make Tibet into a rich, strong and vigorous nation, special privileges and large tracts of property, whether they belong to monasteries or to aristocratic families, should be yielded, and everyone should learn to live with simple people and to help them." I also declared: "Transformations are necessary in every sector. The structure of the government should also be reformed profoundly, so that the people can be more closely connected to the policies of the government and the administration of the country. The task and responsibility of establishing reformed political and religious institutions rest on us all."

The world is rightly concerned about the murders recently committed in the Congo. I too speak up to condemn these attacks, whether they are perpetrated in the Congo, in Algeria, or elsewhere. Yet I still want to ask the world not to forget that thousands of Tibetans were massacred, and are being massacred, solely because they refused to accept foreign domination. The cause of truth and justice should prevail, and at the end of this night of horror and suffering, the dawn of a clear day will rise for Tibet and its people.

I continue to express my profound gratitude to India, Bhutan, Sikkim, and Nepal for the hospitality and kindness with which these neighbors have welcomed us. I would also like to thank the various international and Indian organizations as well as the individuals who have generously helped and aided us. Since large numbers of refugees continue to flow in, I appeal to everyone that they continue to support us as generously as they have done up to now.[15]

———————

On March 10, 1961, the Dalai Lama decided to commemorate the Lhasa insurrection, to honor the sacrifice of the thousands of Tibetans who had protected him against the Chinese threat. Thus, the custom of a solemn gathering on March 10 of every year was established, marked by a speech recapitulating the events of the past year.

The Dalai Lama knows that his words, uttered from the headquarters of the Tibetan government in exile in Dharamsala, will be received and listened to beyond the Himalayas and eagerly read and reread in the Land of the Snows by a people who place all their hopes in him. He also knows that each word of his speech will be analyzed by the Chinese government, and as the years pass he has heard more and more echoes of his statements in the West, where opinion has mobilized for Tibet.

Samdhong Rinpoche relates how carefully the text of the March 10 speeches is worked over and then discussed by the Dalai Lama, as attested by the handwritten drafts, which are full of deletions and emendations.[16]

Since the start of exile, the Dalai Lama has appealed to the world's conscience; in 1963 he deplored the fact that "the community of nations is turning a deaf ear." On September 9, 1959, from exile, he had submitted the Tibetan question to the United Nations, denouncing the violation of his country's independence on a political level and the violation of individual rights, forced labor, massacres, summary executions, and religious persecution on a human level. The General Assembly of the United Nations adopted an initial resolution on October 21, 1959, thanks to Ireland, Malaysia, and Thailand, with the major powers showing no support for Tibet in the context of the Cold War.

The UN's International Commission of Jurists was able to prove that Tibet was a de facto independent state before 1950. Drawing on the Convention for Prevention and Repression of Genocide adopted by the UN in 1948, it wrote a report establishing that China was guilty of the genocide denounced by the Dalai Lama.

In 1960 the Dalai Lama launched a second appeal to the United Nations. For the second time, the General Assembly voted to adopt a resolution noting the violation of human rights in Tibet. Then, in 1965, a third resolution was adopted denouncing the continued violation of the basic rights of Tibetans by China. India, which until then had abstained on the Tibetan question, voted for the resolution that would order China to respect international law. But this resolution remained without effect in the absence of coercive measures on the part of the member states of the UN.

The debate then moved from the General Assembly to the UN's Human Rights Commission, which, in 1991, adopted a resolution denouncing the persistent violation of human rights and liberties in Tibet. Still, after that date the question of human rights in Tibet was no longer added to the agenda of the plenary sessions.

Some idea of the difficulty of the cause defended by the Dalai Lama can be gained when we consider that no country has up to now recognized the Tibetan government in exile, even though a few states have said they favored the membership of the Tibetan Parliament in exile in the Inter-Parliamentary Union.

In the name of humanity, I appeal
to all the peoples of the world

O N MARCH 10, we solemnly commemorate the day the Tibetan people, innocent and unarmed, spontaneously rebelled against the conquest of the Chinese imperialists. Years have passed since that memorable date, but the specter of that macabre tragedy still looms over our holy land. Tyranny and oppression continue, and words cannot describe our sufferings.

Twice the United Nations assembly called for an end to the inhuman behavior against the Tibetans. For my part, many times I have launched appeals for a fair, equitable settlement of this tragedy. But as the International Commission of Jurists recently noted, "neither the resolution of the General Assembly nor any appeals to human conscience have had any effect on the policies of communist China."

The commission, made up of internationally renowned, eminent jurists, also declared that "most of the freedoms proclaimed by the Universal Declaration of Human Rights, including basic, civic, religious, social and economic rights guaranteed by law, are not recognized by the Chinese regime in Tibet." But it is not just from the flagrant violation of human rights and basic freedoms that Tibetans are suffering most today. It is even worse than that. The Chinese authorities in Tibet have denied in actual practice the fact that Tibetans are human beings who possess and experience the sensations and feelings of human beings. Thus, the Tibetans are expelled from their land in favor of Chinese settlements. They are systematically deprived of their sole source of income. In the minds of the Chinese, the life of a Tibetan has no value. It is true that the Chinese authorities vehemently deny these facts. But astonishing proofs of this exist. Thousands of Tibetans have braved the dangers and rigors of a long and dangerous journey to seek asylum in neighboring states. It is certain that if their lives had been even a tiny bit more tolerable, they would not have abandoned their hearths and homes for an uncertain future.

In the present situation, the Tibetans and other peace-loving peoples should call on the world's conscience and protest vigorously against the barbarous and inhuman treatment of the Tibetans by the Chinese invaders.

I want to appeal to all Tibetans to renew their confidence and, once again, to do everything in their power to reestablish peace and freedom in their beloved homeland.

In the name of humanity, I ask all the peoples of the world to come to the aid of the luckless and unfortunate people of Tibet.

I also insist on the extreme danger the current situation presents. We all know that the Chinese armies committed a brutal attack on the territorial integrity of India, despite the efforts of the Indian government to maintain friendly relations with the People's Republic of China.[17] This assault should prove, if there were any need for proof, that so long as the Chinese occupy Tibet, a threat to peace and progress will always loom over the countries of Asia and the Asiatic Southeast. The gravity of the situation was reinforced by Chinese nuclear tests. Until then, the nuclear powers had shown much restraint because they fully realize that the use of the atomic bomb would be disastrous for humanity. Will the Chinese authorities adopt the same restraint once they are in possession of perfectly operational bombs? I fear that we cannot reasonably expect such moderation on the part of a government whose insane ambition knows no God and respects no limits. That is why I sincerely hope and pray that the peoples of the world anticipate the danger that threatens us all.[18]

In this speech on March 10, 1965, the Dalai Lama addressed his people and the world. The Chinese Liberation Army had occupied Tibet supposedly because of the backwardness of its customs and society. The feudal, theocratic system was decried by Mao to justify his work of subjugation, and official propaganda presented Tibetans as primitive, uncultured barbarians. Recently, with lucid realism mingled with sadness, Tenzin Chögyal, the Dalai Lama's younger brother, stated that, for a Chinese person, "killing a Tibetan is less important than killing a rat."

It is true that China established modernization programs in Tibet, but these efforts have been for the exclusive benefit of the Han settlers, who are concentrated in urban zones where they are the majority, at the cost of the Tibetans in rural zones and the nomads, who are hard to control because of their way of life and their attachment to their autonomy.

The nuclear threat mentioned by the Dalai Lama on March 10, 1965, has only grown larger since, and it presents a real danger—both strategic and ecological—for Asia and the world. In the 1990s, with the establishment in the northeast of the country of the Ninth Academy, a high-tech nuclear research center, Tibet has become a military base for China, which has stored one-quarter of its intercontinental missiles with multiple nuclear warheads on the high plateau.

The Roof of the World also serves as a dumping ground for Chinese radioactive waste. The Xinhua Press Agency admitted in 1995 that radioactive pollutants were buried by the shore of Lake Kokonor and in a marsh whose waters empty into the Tsang Chu, which downstream becomes the Yellow River flowing through China. Subsequently, an elevated number of cancer cases has been noted among the nomads, along with an abnormal rate of malformations in animals in the region, where traditional grazing grounds have been shut down.[19]

The Han-ification campaign
in Tibet

THE YEARS OF CHINESE OCCUPATION of Tibet represent a long list of unspoken misfortunes and sufferings. Farmers and livestock owners are deprived of the fruit of their labor. For a meager pittance, large groups of Tibetans are forced to build military roads and fortifications for the Chinese. An incalculable number of our people have been the victims of public trials and purges, where all sorts of humiliations and brutalities have been inflicted on them. The riches of Tibet, accumulated over the course of many centuries, have been taken away to China. A persistent campaign of Han-ification of the Tibetan population continues to be perpetrated, forcibly replacing the Tibetan language with Chinese and changing Tibetan names to words with Chinese sounds. So much for Chinese-style "Tibetan autonomy."

The persecution of Buddhism and Tibetan culture reached a new degree of intensity with the advent of the so-called Cultural Revolution and its by-product, the Red Guard. Monasteries, temples, and even private houses were ransacked, and all religious objects destroyed. Of the countless items that have been destroyed, I will cite the example of a statue of Avalokiteshvara dating from the seventh century. Two heads belonging to it, cut off and mutilated, were secretly taken from Tibet and recently presented to the press in Delhi. Not only has this statue been the object of great veneration over the course of centuries, but it also constitutes a historic, important, and irreplaceable object dear to the Tibetan people. Its destruction is a great loss and a source of profound sadness to us. Recourse to such barbaric methods by insane crowds of immature schoolchildren gave rise to an orgy of senseless vandalism instigated by Mao Tse-tung in the name of the so-called Great Proletarian Cultural Revolution. It was an eloquent proof of the extremities into which Chinese leaders had fallen to try to eliminate the traces of our culture. Humanity and history will certainly condemn the savage massacre of the Tibetan people and the cultural heritage dear to their heart perpetrated by the Chinese.

Observing with profound sadness the terrible poverty and suffering of our people in Tibet, we renewed our firm determination to regain our freedom. During our period of exile, we have all made efforts to prepare ourselves for the day we could return to a Free Tibet. With this aim, we have defined and promulgated a temporary constitution of Tibet, based on the principles of justice, equality, and democracy, in keeping with the teachings of Lord Buddha. It was warmly received by all Tibetans, especially the elected representatives of the Tibetans in exile. We have also launched various programs for reintegration and education, thanks to the sincere sympathy and precious support of the Indian government. Truthfully, my people and I are profoundly grateful to the Indian government for its assistance, which even extended to the safeguarding of our cultural and religious programs. We also thank the different Indian and international organizations that have tirelessly helped us. We continue to need their support, and we confidently hope that it will be granted us as before. We are also grateful to the Indian and foreign governments that have defended the cause of Tibet at the United Nations. Still, given the fact that even the most basic rights of our people are flouted by the Chinese, whom the United Nations has called to order more than once, we believe that peace will not be realizable unless Tibet regains its freedom and is transformed into a demilitarized zone.[20]

In June 1966, Mao launched the Red Guard, which had the mission of destroying "the Four Olds": old ideas, old cultures, old traditions, and old customs. The Cultural Revolution was officially proclaimed in Tibet on August 25, 1966, and the order was given to destroy Tibetan culture in all its forms.

Twenty thousand Red Guards, organized into rival factions, looted and ransacked Lhasa. Monasteries were profaned and their possessions despoiled. To mock faith and piety, religious texts were used to stuff shoes or as toilet paper, printing blocks were made into floorboards, and ritual objects made of precious metal were melted down. The treasures of Tibetan religious art were sent to China to be auctioned off on the international antique market.

The Chinese Communist Party had declared without ambiguity: "Communist ideology and religion are two forces that cannot coexist. The differences between the two are like day and night." All religious practice was forbidden, and the systematic destruction of the monasteries began. Out of all the monks and nuns, who represented close to one-quarter of the population, more than eleven thousand were tortured to death, and half were forcibly defrocked or forced to have sexual intercourse in public.

The Tibetan population was submitted to self-criticism and reeducation meetings, where workers had to confront their bosses, farmers their landowners, students their professors, and monks their abbots. Confessions were torn from them by extremely violent methods, some resulting in summary executions.

The years from 1966 to 1979 represent, for the Tibetans, the cruelest period of Chinese occupation. As the Dalai Lama lamented, Tibetan identity was attacked even down to its language. Experts created a "Sino-Tibetan language of friendship" that distorted Tibetan language with Chinese expressions.

Five hundred Tibetans
perished while fleeing their
occupied country

THE COMMEMORATION ON MARCH 10 has become sacred for all Tibetans, and it is an important date in the historic struggle of our people, who want to free themselves from their oppressors. It was on this day that the Tibetans courageously tried to free themselves from the yoke of Chinese leaders. In 1950 the Chinese occupied our country by force, exercising an ambiguous, obsolete claim of suzerainty. Compared to the superiority of the Chinese forces, our resistance was condemned in advance, and it led to a large-scale massacre of thousands of our fellow citizens. But the spirit of a people that believes in human dignity and in the freedom of all nations, large and small, cannot let itself be broken by an aggressor, however powerful. On that fatal day, our entire country joined together to defy the Chinese, and we reasserted our national identity in clear terms for the outside world. Our people's struggle is continuing today both inside and outside Tibet.

For our compatriots who have remained in Tibet, the battle is both a physical and a moral one. The Chinese have used every trick possible, along with force, to break the Tibetans' resistance. The fact that they have not succeeded is admitted by China and attested to by the many Tibetans who flee to India and other neighboring countries each year, despite increasingly severe controls imposed by the Chinese Communists at the borders.

In 1968, almost five hundred Tibetans perished as they were trying to flee to India. They knew that their chances of success were almost nonexistent, and yet they preferred to take this risk. Is it conceivable that a people can reach such suicidal extremes when it is supposedly satisfied with the regime it is living under, according to the Chinese Communists?

During each of the years that have gone by, the Chinese have successively tried to indoctrinate thousands of Tibetan children, forcibly separating them from their parents and sending them to China. In that country, they have been kept away from all Tibetan culture, taught the doctrines of Mao, and forced to mock and ridicule the Tibetan way of life. But contrary to Chinese expectations, a large majority of them are now resisting the regime forcibly imposed on Tibet. So long as human beings have the ability to think, and so long as they seek the truth, the Chinese Communists will not completely succeed at indoctrinating our children. There is no doubt that the fate reserved for annexed ethnic minorities attests to Han chauvinism. However, far from managing to reach their goals, the Chinese are only feeding the nationalist flame. It is for this reason that even young Tibetan Communists have joined forces with the rest of the country against the Chinese.

The culture and religious beliefs of our country have been one of the main targets of Communist repression. The destruction of monastic universities, cultural centers, and other similar institutions begun in the beginning of the Chinese conquest has recently intensified with the Cultural Revolution and the founding of the Red Guard. Monks, nuns, and scholars have been expelled from monasteries and cultural institutions. Large numbers of the local population are being forced to build an immense network of strategic roads in Tibet, which has become a huge military base at the borders of neighboring countries. This poses a growing threat to the peace of these regions.

It has been up to those of us who were lucky enough to flee the Chinese Communists to take up the noble task for which so many of our compatriots have given their lives. Our people in exile are conscientiously trying to prepare for the day we can return to a Free Tibet. Thus, Tibetan children, whom I regard as the cornerstone of a future free, independent Tibet, are receiving the best chances possible to develop and grow mentally and morally to become men and women profoundly rooted in their own culture, beliefs, and way of life, while still remaining close to modern civilization and enriched by the greatest accomplishments of world culture. They will thus be healthy, creative Tibetan citizens, capable of serving our nation and humanity. Our wish is not only to be able to contribute to the prosperity of our host country but also to act in such a way that an authentically Tibetan culture can take root and flourish outside of Tibet, until we are able to return there. Returning one day is a hope that will always accompany us, and an aim toward which we must ceaselessly work.[21]

The ability of Tibetans to escape their situation, as mentioned by the Dalai Lama on March 10, 1968, has scarcely changed today. The events of September 2006 were a tragic reminder of this: Chinese border guards attacked a column of seventy-five Tibetans trying to reach Nepal by the Nangpa La Pass, 5,700 meters high, at the foot of Mount Cho Oyu.

The patrol aimed and shot at sight in a snow field. Kelsang Namtso, a seventeen-year-old Tibetan nun, collapsed, pierced with bullets. Her companions were unable to carry her body, for fear of being arrested. The next day a few soldiers returned and threw the body into a crevasse, under the eyes of some Danish mountain climbers.

During the fusillade, a twenty-year-old man, Kunsang Namgyal, was wounded and made prisoner along with thirty other Tibetans, including fourteen children who lost their lives.

The incident had witnesses: from their base camp, mountain climbers of different nationalities filmed the soldiers shooting, then pursuing and arresting the people fleeing. The images were quickly uploaded to the Internet and broadcast on television, provoking protests in several countries.

Far from the cameras, beneath the cloak of silence imposed by Chinese authorities, Tibetans have been experiencing such tragedies for the half-century of their country's occupation. To give their children a Tibetan education and allow them to escape forced sinicization, parents place their babies into the arms of older children, whom they entrust to smugglers. They make the sacrifice of separating from them so that the children can grow up to be proud of being Tibetan.

The fleeing children must ascend the highest mountains in the world, through barriers of snow and ice that reach 7,000 or 8,000 meters. To cross the passes, they must travel in temperatures that can fall to 20 degrees below zero, without the protection of suitable clothing, without adequate nourishment, and at the risk of being suddenly discovered by Chinese patrols. Some die of cold. Some die of hunger. In these icy solitudes, they fall and cannot stand up again. Others reach the end of their journey at the cost of unheard-of efforts.

Tenzin Tsendu, a poet and freedom fighter, is the author of Border Passage, a text that evokes the ordeal of a Tibetan mother accompanying her children to freedom in exile:

> Silently threading our way by night and hiding by day,
> In twenty days we reached the snow-covered mountains.
> The border was still many days away by foot.
> The rocky ground scraped our bodies, bent from effort and pain.

Over our heads a bomber passed
My children shouted in terror
And huddled against my chest.
I was so exhausted I felt as if I had no limbs,
But my mind was watchful. . . .
We had to press ahead or we would die on the spot.
One daughter here, one son there,
A baby on my back,
We reached the snow fields.
We climbed up the side of monster-like mountains
Whose snowy banks often cover the bodies of travelers who
  ventured here.
In the midst of these snow-white fields of death,
A pile of frozen corpses
Awoke our wavering courage.
Drops of blood were scattered on the snow.
Soldiers must have crossed their path,
In our own country they had fallen into the hands of the
  Red Dragon.
We pray to the Wish-fulfilling Jewel,
Hope in our hearts, prayer on our lips,
We have almost nothing left to eat
And only the ice to quench our thirst,
We climb together, night after night.
But one night, my daughter complained her foot was burning.
She fell and stood up on her frozen leg.
Her skin was tattered and gashed with deep, bleeding cuts,
She curled up, shivering with pain.
The next day, both her legs were lost.
Assailed by death on every side,

I was a powerless mother;
"Amala, save my brothers,
I'm going to rest a little."
Until I no longer heard her moans lost in the distance,
I looked behind me, through my tears and the torture of this pain.
My legs carried me, but my mind remained with her.
For a long time afterwards, in exile, I continue to see her
Waving her frozen hands at me.
The oldest of my children, but barely a teenager,
Leaving our country was an ordeal.
Every night I light a butter lamp for her,
And her brothers join me in prayer.[22]

Tibet, Sanctuary of Peace for the World

My people's contribution to world peace

THE WORLD HAS BECOME more and more interdependent, so that a lasting peace on the national, regional, and global levels is possible only if we take the interests of all people into account. In our time, it is crucial that we all, strong and weak alike, contribute our share. As the leader of the Tibetan people and as a Buddhist monk, I am devoted to the principles of a religion based on love and compassion. Above all, I am a human being, since it is my fate to share this planet with all of you, my brothers and sisters. As the world is growing smaller, we need one another more than we ever did in the past. This is true for all parts of the world, including the continent I come from.

These days, in Asia as well as elsewhere, tensions are high. There are open conflicts in the Middle East, in southeastern Asia, and in my own country, Tibet. To a great extent, these problems are the symptom of underlying tensions that exist in the major powers' spheres of influence.

In order to resolve regional conflicts, we must take into account the respective interests of all the countries and peoples concerned, large and small. Without global solutions that include the aspirations of the peoples most directly concerned, half-measures or expedients will only create additional problems. The Tibetans want keenly to contribute to peace, both on a regional and a world level, and they think that they are in a unique position to do so. Traditionally, we are a nonviolent people who love peace. Ever since Buddhism was introduced to Tibet over a thousand years ago, Tibetans have practiced nonviolence and respected all forms of life. We have extended this attitude to our country's international relations. Tibet's highly strategic position in the heart of Asia, between the great powers of the continent, historically confers on us an essential role in maintaining peace and stability. It is precisely for this reason that, in the past, Asian empires have taken care to stay out of Tibet by mutual agreement. The value of Tibet as an independent buffer state was perceived as an ingredient for stability in the region.

When the newly formed People's Republic of China invaded Tibet in 1950, a new source of conflict emerged. This was brought out when, following the national Tibetan uprising against the Chinese and my flight to India in 1959, tensions between China and India increased, which resulted in a border war in 1962. In 1987, once again, large military units massed on both sides of the Himalayan border, and tension was once again running dangerously high.

What was actually in question was not the boundary line between India and Tibet, but the unlawful Chinese occupation of Tibet, which has given China direct access to the Indian subcontinent. Chinese authorities have tried to downplay the problem by stating that Tibet has always been a part of China. This is not true. Tibet was a fully independent state when it was invaded by the People's Liberation Army in 1950.

Ever since the Tibetan emperors unified Tibet over a thousand years ago, our country has been able to defend its independence, until the middle of the twentieth century. Tibet in the past extended its influence over neighboring countries and peoples, and in later times it came under the domination of powerful foreign rulers: the Khans of Mongolia, the Gurkhas of Nepal, the Manchu emperors, and the British present in India.

Of course, it is not rare for states to undergo foreign influence or interference. So-called satellite relations are perhaps the most convincing example of this—great nations exercising their influence over less powerful allies or neighbors. As studies carried out by the highest legal authorities have shown, in the case of Tibet the occasional submission of our country to foreign influences has never implied a loss of its independence. And it is incontestable that at the time of the invasion of the Communist armies of Beijing, Tibet was from every standpoint an independent state.

Chinese aggression, condemned by almost all nations of the free world, constituted a flagrant violation of international law. As the military occupation of Tibet continues, the world should remember that, even if the Tibetans have lost their freedom, according to international law, the Tibet of today is still an independent state occupied illegally.

I am not trying to get involved in a political or legal argument over the status of Tibet. My wish is merely to emphasize the obvious and indisputable fact that as Tibetans, we are a distinct people with our own culture, language, religion, and history. Without Chinese occupation, Tibet would keep its role as a buffer state, thus protecting and guaranteeing the promotion of peace in Asia.

Despite the holocaust inflicted on our people through the past decades of Chinese occupation, I have always tried to reach a solution through direct, frank discussions with the Chinese. In 1982, following the change in the Chinese leadership, and thanks to direct contacts with the Beijing government, I sent my representatives to initiate talks on the future of my country and my people.

We began the dialogue with an open, positive attitude, eager to take into consideration the legitimate needs of the People's Republic of China. I hoped that this attitude would be reciprocal and that a solution would eventually be found to satisfy and preserve the aspirations and interests of both parties. Unfortunately, China continued to respond to our efforts in a defensive way, taking our detailed report of the very real difficulties in Tibet merely as criticisms of its regime.

But there is worse yet. In our opinion, the Chinese government has allowed the chance for real dialogue to pass by. Instead of dealing with the real problems of six million Tibetans, it has tried to reduce the whole Tibetan question to my own personal status.

It is my most sincere wish, and that of the Tibetan people, to restore to Tibet its invaluable historic role by once again converting the entire country, including the three provinces of U-Tsang, Kham, and Amdo, into a zone of stability, peace, and harmony. In the purest Buddhist tradition, Tibet would thereby offer its services and hospitality to all those who defend world peace, the good of humanity, and concern for the natural environment we all share.[23]

It was in 1987 that the Dalai Lama gave this speech to the Human Rights Commission of the U.S. Congress. After Mao's death, Deng Xiaoping had enacted a policy of generally easing restrictions in Tibet, beginning in 1979. The Chinese Communist Party called together a first Work Symposium on Tibet in the spring of 1980 and sent Hu Yaobang, general secretary of the

Chinese Communist Party, to evaluate the situation in Tibet. Shocked by the great poverty of Tibetan society, when he returned he suggested the radical reforms of decollectivizing property, granting greater autonomy, and decreasing taxes. It was decided that the number of Chinese administrators would be reduced by two-thirds, leaving the country's management to the Tibetans themselves, who would be charged with reviving their culture. Political prisoners, imprisoned since 1959, were released, and the Chinese Communist Party invited exiles, notably the Dalai Lama, to return to the country to "take part in the socialist reconstruction."

The Tibetan government in exile sent three investigative missions to Tibet in 1979 and 1980. Their visit aroused popular jubilation that surpassed in fervor anything the Chinese could have imagined. The Dalai Lama's brothers and sisters were present, and their compatriots rushed at them to touch them and tear off pieces of their clothing, which were carried as relics. These pieces of cloth were precious, for they came from people who were close to their exiled spiritual leader, for whom their veneration had not flagged. Twenty years of indoctrination and brutal repression had not shaken their faith, much to the chagrin of the Communist forces. The second visit was cut short because the crowd in Lhasa became uncontrollable.

In September 1980, the Dalai Lama offered to send fifty teachers from the community in exile to teach in Tibet. He offered to open a liaison office in Beijing to reestablish confidence, but China equivocated.

In March 1981, the Dalai Lama took note of this in a letter to Deng Xiaoping, while still insisting that teachers be swiftly authorized to lead their educative mission in Tibet. A few months later, in July, Hu Yaobang replied, asking the Dalai Lama to return to Lhasa, where he could enjoy the same political status and the same conditions of life as before 1959.

It was to this new context that the Dalai Lama alluded when he mentioned the representatives sent by his government in 1982 and 1984 to Beijing. But disappointment lay in store for them, since the Chinese uncompromisingly declared that they wanted to discuss only one single point: "the unconditional return of the Dalai Lama to the motherland."

The period of liberalization, which had allowed for a resurgence of the Tibetan way of life and religion, did not last long. In 1984 a second Work Symposium on Tibet called the leadership of Hu Yaobang into question, criticizing him for allowing Tibetan nationalism to be reborn. He was dismissed as the head of the Communist Party, and once again, Chinese policies became stricter. This was when the Dalai Lama, at the invitation of the U.S. Congress, decided to bring the Tibetan cause onto the international scene—accompanied by a message of peace for the world.

I propose that Tibet become a sanctuary of *ahimsa* for the world

I PROPOSE THAT ALL OF TIBET, including the eastern provinces of Kham and Amdo, be transformed into a zone of *ahimsa*, a Hindu term designating a state of nonviolence and peace.

The establishment of such a zone of peace would be in keeping with the historic role of Tibet, a peaceful, neutral Buddhist nation and buffer zone between the great powers of the continent. It would also be in keeping with Nepal's proposal to become a zone of peace, a project that was publicly approved by China. The Nepalese peace zone would have a much stronger impact if it included Tibet and the neighboring regions.

Establishing a zone of peace in Tibet would force a withdrawal of Chinese troops and military installations. It would also allow India to withdraw its troops and military camps from the border regions in the Himalayas. An international agreement could guarantee China's legitimate need for security and build relations of trust between Tibetans, Indians, Chinese, and the other peoples of the region. It would be to everyone's advantage, especially China and India. Their security would be reinforced, and it would lighten the economic burden involved in maintaining large concentrations of troops on the disputed Himalayan border.

Throughout history, relations between China and India have never been tense. It was only when the Chinese armies invaded Tibet, thereby creating for the first time a common border, that tensions appeared between the two powers, resulting in the war of 1962. Since then, many dangerous incidents have occurred. The reestablishment of good relations between the two most populous nations in the world would be greatly eased if they were separated, as was the case in the past, by a vast, friendly buffer zone.

To improve relations between the Tibetan and Chinese peoples, the first step is the restoration of trust. After the holocaust of recent decades—in the course of which over a million Tibetans, or one-sixth of our population, lost their lives, while at least the same number languished in concentration camps because of their religious beliefs and their love of freedom—only a withdrawal of Chinese troops could initiate a real process of reconciliation. The large occupation force in Tibet reminds the Tibetans every day of the oppression and suffering they are all undergoing. Removal of the troops would be a strong signal letting us hope that in the future a relationship of friendship and trust could be established with the Chinese.[24]

The transformation of Tibet into a zone of peace dedicated to the culture of ahimsa (nonviolence) was suggested by the Dalai Lama in his September 1987 speech before the Human Rights Commission of the U.S. Congress, in which he presented his Five-Point Peace Plan. The spiritual leader developed the argument that peace in Tibet could guarantee peace in the world, according to the principle of interdependence dear to him. This speech marked an important turning point in the analysis of the Tibetan situation by the Dalai Lama and the Tibetan government in exile.

Until 1979, the central Tibetan administration and the Tibetan people had tried to recover Tibet's independence by calling on the United Nations, without much success, to recognize the historic sovereignty of their country, which, contrary to what Chinese propaganda asserts, was never part of China. While acknowledging that the world was becoming more and more interdependent politically, militarily, and economically, the Dalai Lama decided to put all his efforts into resolving the question of Tibet through dialogue and negotiation.

In 1979 Deng Xiaoping had decreed that anything about Tibet could be discussed except its independence. During meetings with members of the Kashag, the Dalai Lama studied the possibility of satisfying the aspirations of the Tibetan people while still accepting the idea that Tibet would become a Chinese province, provided a real status of self-management and autonomy were granted it. The incontrovertible condition to make this autonomy effective was to annul the administrative division of the country, arbitrarily imposed by the occupier, into five zones attached to Chinese provinces. The Dharamsala government proposed that all territories be reunified into one administrative entity to be self-managed democratically. Such measures would allow the preservation of Tibetan religion and culture by giving Tibetans the power to decide their own socioeconomic development. China would remain responsible for defense, foreign affairs, education, and the economy. It would gain the advantage of a long-term stability by preserving its territorial integrity. Tibetans would then have no more reason to demand their independence.

These points form the basis of the policy called "the Middle Way," conceived to be mutually beneficial to both parties and to serve peace in the world. It is still advocated by the Dalai Lama in his negotiations with the government of the People's Republic of China. He gave a complete account of this a year after his 1987 speech in the United States when he addressed the European Parliament in Strasbourg.

In the name of the spiritual heritage of my people

W E ARE LIVING TODAY in a very interdependent world. One single nation cannot solve its problems by itself. If we don't realize universal responsibility, our very survival is in danger. That is why I have always believed in the necessity for better understanding, closer cooperation, and greater respect among the nations of the world. The European Parliament is an inspiring example. Having emerged from the chaos of war, the enemies of yesterday, in a single generation, learned to coexist and cooperate.

Tibet is going through a very difficult period. Tibetans, especially those who are undergoing Chinese occupation, aspire to freedom and justice as well as to a future they themselves can determine, so as to safeguard fully their singular identity and live in peace with their neighbors. For over a thousand years, the Tibetans have adhered to spiritual values, defending the region's ecology so as to maintain the delicate balance of life on the high plateau. Inspired by the Buddha's message of nonviolence and compassion, protected by our mountains, we have tried to respect all forms of life and to abandon war as an instrument of national policy.

Throughout our history, going back over two thousand years, we have been independent. At no point since the foundation of our nation in 127 BC have we ceded our sovereignty to a foreign power. As is the case for all nations, Tibet has gone through periods when its neighbors—Mongols, Manchus, Chinese, the English, and the Nepalese Gurkhas—have tried to subjugate it. These were brief episodes that the Tibetan people have never agreed to interpret as a loss of national sovereignty. In fact, there were times when the kings of Tibet conquered vast territories in China and other neighboring states. But this does not mean that we Tibetans claim these territories now.

In 1949 the People's Republic of China invaded Tibet by force. Since then, Tibet has endured the most somber period in its history. Over a million of our people have perished as a result of the occupation. Thousands of monasteries have been reduced to rubble. A generation has grown up deprived of education, economic development, and national identity. Although the Chinese leaders have put certain reforms into effect, they have also brought about a massive population transfer of ethnic Chinese to the Tibetan plateau. This policy has already reduced the six million Tibetans to the condition of a minority.

I have always forbidden my people to resort to violence in their efforts to put an end to their sufferings. I do believe, however, that a people has every moral right to protest against injustice. Unfortunately, demonstrations in Tibet have been violently repressed by the Chinese police and army. I will continue to advise nonviolence, but unless China abandons its brutal methods, the Tibetans cannot be held responsible for an aggravation of the situation.

Every Tibetan hopes and prays for the complete restoration of their nation's independence. Thousands of our people have sacrificed their lives, and our entire country has suffered in this fight. But the Chinese have entirely failed to recognize the aspirations of the Tibetan people, and they persist in their policy of brutal repression.

I have thought for a long time about a realistic solution that could put an end to my country's tragedy. With the Kashag, I have solicited the opinions of many friends and concerned persons. On September 21, 1987, before the Human Rights Commission in the Congress in Washington, I announced a Five-Point Peace Plan in which I called for the transformation of Tibet into a zone of peace, a sanctuary where humanity and nature could live together in harmony. I also called for the respect of human rights and democratic ideals, for the protection of the environment, and for the end of Chinese population transfers to Tibet.

The fifth point of the Peace Plan called for serious negotiations between Tibetans and Chinese. We took the initiative in expressing these thoughts, which, we hope, could solve the Tibetan question. All of Tibet, known under the name of Chokha Sum (including the provinces of U-Tsang, Kham, and Amdo), should become a self-managed, democratic, law-abiding entity, with the people agreeing to work for the common good and the protection of the environment, in association with the People's Republic of China. The Chinese government would remain responsible for Tibet's foreign policy. The Tibetan government, for its part, would develop and maintain relations, through its own foreign affairs bureau, in the sectors of business, education, culture, religion, tourism, science, sports, and other nonpolitical activities.

Since individual freedom is the true source of development for any society, the government of Tibet will try to ensure this freedom by fully adhering to the Universal Declaration of Human Rights, understanding the rights of freedom of expression, peaceful assembly, and religion. Since religion represents Tibet's national source of identity, and since spiritual values are at the heart of the rich Tibetan culture, it would be the Tibetan government's special task to safeguard and develop them.

The Tibetan government should pass strict laws to protect wild flora and fauna. Exploitation of natural resources will be carefully controlled. The production, experimentation, and storing of nuclear weapons and of any other arms will be forbidden, along with the use of nuclear energy and technologies that produce dangerous waste. It will be the task of the Tibetan government to transform Tibet into the largest nature preserve on our planet. A regional peace conference will be called to ensure that Tibet becomes an authentic, completely demilitarized sanctuary of peace. In order to create an atmosphere of trust favorable to fruitful negotiations, the Chinese government should immediately stop its human rights violations in Tibet and abandon its policy of transferring Chinese people to Tibet.

Those are the ideas I continue to have in mind. I am aware that many Tibetans are disappointed with this moderate position. No doubt there will continue to be many discussions within our own community, both in Tibet and in exile. That is an essential and unavoidable step in every process of change. I believe that these reflections represent the most realistic way to reestablish a specific Tibetan identity and to restore Tibetans' basic rights, while still allowing for Chinese interests. I would, however, like to stress that, whatever the outcome of negotiations with the Chinese may be, the Tibetan people should have the final word in any decision. Consequently, any proposal will contain a plan for a full-scale legal process to define the wishes of the Tibetan people by way of a national referendum.

I do not wish to take an active part in the government of Tibet. Nevertheless, I will continue to work as much as I can for the wellbeing and happiness of Tibetans, so long as it is necessary.

We are ready to present a proposal to the government of the People's Republic of China based on these considerations. A negotiating team representing the Tibetan government in exile has been appointed. We are ready to meet the Chinese to discuss the details of such a proposal, with the aim of arriving at a fair solution.

We are encouraged by the profound interest our cause arouses in an increasing number of governments and political leaders. We are reassured in our position by the recent changes in China, which have brought a group of new, more pragmatic, and more liberal leaders into power.

We pray that the Chinese government and leaders will examine the ideas I have expounded seriously and in detail. Only dialogue and a desire to analyze the Tibetan reality with honesty and lucidity can lead to a viable solution. We hope we can conduct discussions with the Chinese government while keeping the general interest of humanity in mind. Thus, our proposal will be made with a wish for conciliation, and we hope for the same attitude on the part of the Chinese.

The unique history of my country and its profound spiritual heritage make it perfectly apt to fill the role of a peace sanctuary in the heart of Asia. Its historic status as a neutral buffer zone, contributing to the stability of the entire continent, deserves to be restored. Peace and security in Asia, and throughout the whole world, will thus be reinforced. In the future, it will no longer be necessary for Tibet to remain an occupied, forcibly oppressed country, unproductive and marked by suffering. It can become a free paradise where humanity and nature will live in harmonious balance and a creative model for the resolution of the tensions afflicting many regions of the world.

The Chinese leaders should realize that, in the occupied territories, colonial rule is anachronistic. An authentic union of several countries is possible on a large scale only on the basis of freely consenting adherence, when the result that is aimed for satisfies all parties concerned. The European Union is an eloquent example of this.

The solution of the Tibetan problem, as we have proposed it, will be beneficial not only to the Tibetan and Chinese peoples but also to the peace and stability of the region and the world.[25]

———

In September 1987, when the Dalai Lama had presented his Five-Point Peace Plan to the Human Rights Commission of the U.S. Congress, he asked that "China engage seriously in negotiations to solve the relative question of the future status of Tibet."

In June 1988, addressing the European Parliament in Strasbourg, the Dalai Lama expounded on his plan, which included an agreement to renounce a claim for the independence for Tibet in favor of an effective autonomy. This major concession aimed at bringing about the creation of a democratic political entity of self-management for all three provinces of Tibet, which would remain attached to the People's Republic of China, with the Chinese government continuing to manage Tibet's foreign policy and defense. The Strasbourg proposal was based on the idea of creating, in the spirit of the Tibetan way of life, a sanctuary in Tibet dedicated to world peace and founded on spiritual development and the promotion of the human values of love, compassion, nonviolence, tolerance, and forgiveness. According to Samdhong Rinpoche, the Dalai Lama gave up the claim to independence because he was concerned about allowing a real revival of the spiritual and cultural heritage of Buddhism, regarded as humanity's global inheritance, before it was too late.[26]

But the People's Republic of China declared that the Strasbourg proposal was only a claim of independence under cover of autonomy and that the Dalai Lama was pursuing the idea of separating Tibet from the "motherland." Officials insulted him by calling him a "leader of a separatist clique." And in 1988, in Lhasa, peaceful protests of monks and nuns were barbarously repressed, arousing international outrage. In March 1989, new demonstrations were put down by the army. Over one hundred people were killed, and three thousand were imprisoned. Martial law was established and kept in place for over a year, until May 1990.

These events led to an unprecedented mobilization of public opinion in Western capitals. The Tibetan cause was no longer the internal problem the Chinese regime wanted to reduce it to, since it now concerned the world. The Dalai Lama had become credible as a spokesman not only for his people but for the world's conscience by suggesting that Tibet, today a land of suffering and genocide, be transformed into a sanctuary of peace.

My weapons are truth, courage, and determination

TODAY, WHEN I ENVISAGE the future of Tibet, I cannot help but think about certain landmark events. In China the popular movement for democracy was crushed in Tiananmen Square in June 1989 with a violence that was unbridled. But I do not believe that those demonstrations were in vain. On the contrary, the spirit of freedom was rekindled among the Chinese, and China cannot ignore the impact of this spirit of freedom that wafted through many parts of the world.

Extraordinary changes were under way in Eastern Europe, events that set the tone for a social and political renewal throughout the world. Similarly, Namibia regained its independence from South Africa, and the South African government made its first step toward abolishing apartheid. It is encouraging to note that these changes stemmed from authentic popular movements and that they are linked to the irrepressible human desire for freedom and justice. These historic changes indicate that reason, courage, determination, and the inextinguishable need for freedom will end up carrying the day.

That is why I am urging the Chinese leaders not to resist the wave of change, but to examine the problems of the Tibetan and Chinese peoples with imagination and an open mind. I believe that repression will never crush the determination of a people to live in freedom and dignity. The Chinese leaders should look at China's internal problems and the Tibetan question with a new eye and a fresh state of mind. Before it is too late, they must listen to the voice of reason, nonviolence, and moderation spoken by the Tibetan people.

Despite the claims of Chinese propaganda, millions of non-Chinese residents, living in regions presently controlled by the People's Republic, are enduring all sorts of discrimination. The Chinese themselves admit that, despite years of the Communist regime, these regions have remained backward and poor. However, the most serious impact of Chinese policy on the peoples of these regions is the demographic transformation that has been imposed on them. Almost everywhere, new Chinese immigrants have become the majority. Manchuria has been completely absorbed. In inner Mongolia, only 2.6 million Mongols remain, surrounded by 18 million new Chinese arrivals. Over 50 percent of the population of eastern Turkistan is Chinese today, whereas in Tibet the 6 million Tibetans are outnumbered by 7.5 million Chinese immigrants.

Naturally, the non-Chinese peoples are rebellious. Unless the Chinese leaders take measures to appease them, it is very likely that serious problems will arise in the future. I believe it is imperative that China try to solve these questions through dialogue and compromise. The government of China must realize that these questions in the non-Chinese regions under its yoke are not purely economic ones. They are at root political, and as such, they can be resolved only by decisions of a political order.

To bring a peaceful, reasonable solution to the Tibetan question, I revealed my Five-Point Peace Plan and presented the Strasbourg Proposal. Even after the proclamation of martial law in Tibet, we suggested that preliminary meetings take place in Hong Kong, in order to discuss the steps to follow to reduce tensions and facilitate actual negotiations. Unfortunately, the Chinese leaders, to this day, have not replied positively to our sincere efforts.

The Chinese rejected and vehemently condemned my position on the past status and history of Tibet. They want to see me change my position. But it is not possible to alter the truth of the facts. In their narrowness of mind, the Chinese did not understand the gist of the message I tried to pass on to them in my Five-Point Peace Plan, in my Strasbourg Proposal, or in my Nobel speech concerning future relations between Tibet and China, which I am ready to examine with an open mind through dialogue.

Just as we struggle for the rights, freedom, and future well-being of six million Tibetans, so we should reinforce our democratic institutions and our process of democratization. As I have declared many times, the respect for freedom and democracy is essential for the development of a modern Tibet. In 1963 I approved the Democratic Constitution of Tibet, and we have acquired significant experience in the functioning of democratic institutions. It is still necessary to democratize further, both in the Assembly of Deputies of the Tibetan People and in the Tibetan Administration. That is why I have collected the opinions and suggestions of our people. I feel it is the responsibility of every Tibetan to create a completely free and democratic community in exile.

It is important that the Chinese authorities recognize the real aspirations of the Tibetan people, the majority of whom live in Tibet. Almost all Tibetans wish for nothing other than the full-fledged independence of their country. If the Chinese doubt this, they should authorize a referendum controlled by an international commission in Tibet to determine the aspirations of the Tibetan people.

I note with sadness that far from examining the Tibetan question from a new perspective, the Chinese authorities continue to use their impressive military power to crush the many demonstrations of Tibetans. Despite such brutality, the Tibetans in Tibet remain determined and unwavering. It is the responsibility of every Tibetan to struggle for freedom and human rights. But our struggle should be based on nonviolence.

One important event was the Nobel Peace Prize I was awarded. Although it did not change my status as a simple monk, I was happy about it for the Tibetan people, for that prize brought a deserved recognition of their struggle for freedom and justice. It reaffirmed our conviction that with the weapons of truth, courage, and determination, we will succeed at freeing our country. The relationship between Tibet and China should be based on the principle of equality, trust, and mutual benefit. It should also be based on the recommendations that the sovereigns of Tibet and China wisely expounded in a treaty made in AD 823. According to the clause engraved on a stone column in Lhasa, "The Tibetans will live happily in vast Tibet, and the Chinese in vast China."[27]

In March 1990, "a spirit of freedom [was] wafting throughout the world" in Europe, with the fall of the Berlin Wall and the dismantling of the Soviet Union, and in China, with the demonstrations on Tiananmen Square, but in Tibet martial law was still in effect. It would not be lifted until a few months later, in May. But this measure did not signify the end of the oppression, whose brutality only increased, as an Amnesty International report noted in 1991.

Beginning in 1992, special teams were charged with searching private houses throughout all of Tibet. People who owned photos, books, or teachings of the Dalai Lama were arrested and cruelly tortured, then imprisoned. Many of them disappeared.

In 1994 Beijing passed a series of measures to eradicate Tibetan opposition. The third Work Symposium on Tibet advocated ensuring "the unity of the motherland and fighting against separatism." In the rhetoric of the propaganda of the "anti-Dalai" and "anti-separatism" campaigns, it was a question of "a life-and-death struggle," and the recommendation was to "tirelessly rain down blows for public safety." An escalade of violence ensued throughout all of Tibet, reminiscent of the worst times in the Cultural Revolution; in July 1996 the Communist Party launched three major political campaigns called "Patriotic Education," "Spiritual Civilization," and "Hit Hard." With much propaganda, the first two initiatives aimed at eliminating the Tibetan religion, culture, and language: "We must teach Buddhists to reform themselves to answer the need for stability in Tibet and to adapt to the socialist model." To supervise monks and nuns, regarded as dangerous elements who led separatist activities in the name of the Dalai Lama, Committees of Democratic Administration and Patriotic Work Units were established in all monasteries. In 1998 this policy led to the expulsion of almost ten thousand monks and nuns, and the assistant secretary of the Communist Party declared that thirty-five thousand monks and nuns had been reformed thanks to the campaigns of patriotic reeducation.

With the "Hit Hard" campaign, the authorities undertook to eradicate all trace of "Tibetan political activism." This expression covered such activities as speaking to foreigners, owning publications of the Tibetan government in exile or photos of the Dalai Lama, and participating in peaceful demonstrations. People were forced to give information on their neighbors, colleagues, or parents, under penalty of losing their houses or jobs. Suspects were imprisoned, and confessions were wrested from them under torture. Many died as a result of ill treatment. In 1999 a commission of doctors seeking to uphold human rights established that in Tibet torture was used more and more as a substitute for the death penalty. A slow death or a degradation of individuals' lives resulted from this practice.

In the decade from 1990 to 2000, new interrogation and detention centers were built throughout Tibet. Thanks to the testimonies of political prisoners, some of whom managed to buy instruments of torture from their guards in exchange for gold, the different techniques of torture were cataloged by organizations affiliated with the UN, such as the International Commission of Jurists, the Workgroup on Arbitrary Detention, and the special report on torture.

Besides flouting human rights, Chinese authorities initiated a new policy of massive Han population transfer to Tibet with the launching of a program called "Development of the West." That program has only accelerated since the turn of the millennium as it takes advantage of the infrastructures that facilitate the transport of new settlements, like the railroad connecting Lhasa to Beijing, inaugurated on July 1, 2006.

The Dalai Lama has called this a policy of "demographic aggression" that reduces Tibetans to no more than a minority in their ancestral land and that aims to incorporate Tibet once and for all into China: "A real demographic aggression is occurring, and this is an extremely serious problem. Today the population of Lhasa, according to the latest census reports, is two-thirds Chinese. This is also the case in all the main cities in Tibet where Tibetans have become the minority. The Tibetans in India are more Tibetan than the Tibetans in Tibet."

In April 2000, the European Parliament voted on a resolution expressing keen concern for the threat that "the massive transfer of Han Chinese to Tibet posed to the cultural and spiritual heritage of Tibet." The deputies urged China to undertake a dialogue "without preconditions" with the Dalai Lama on the basis of the Five-Point Peace Plan and to put an end to its "persistent and aggravated violation of the basic freedoms of the Tibetan people."

Tibet is still suffering from flagrant, unimaginable human rights violations

I CONTINUE TO OFFER MY PRAYERS, and pay homage to all those courageous men and women in Tibet who endured immense ordeals and sacrificed their lives for the cause of our people. I express my solidarity with the Tibetans who are at present enduring repression and ill treatment. I salute both the Tibetans in Tibet and Tibetans abroad, those who support our cause, and all defenders of justice.

For six decades, Tibetans throughout all of Tibet, known under the name of Chokha Sum (including the provinces of U-Tsang, Kham, and Amdo), have been forced to live in a constant state of fear, intimidation, and suspicion, subject to Chinese repression. Still, the Tibetan people have been able to maintain their religious faith, their firm sense of nationality, and their unique culture, while still keeping alive their age-old aspiration for freedom. I have great admiration for these qualities in our people and for their indomitable courage. They make me feel great pride and satisfaction.

Many governments, nongovernmental organizations, and individuals throughout the world, faithful to the ideal of peace and justice, have steadily supported the cause of Tibet. Over the course of recent years, governments and peoples of numerous countries have made important gestures to show their solidarity clearly, and I would like to express my gratitude to them.

The very complex problem of Tibet is linked to other questions having to do with politics, society, law, human rights, religion, culture, national identity, the economy, and the natural environment. That is why a global approach must be adopted to resolve it by taking into account the interests of all parties involved, rather than one single faction. So we have been firm in our engagement in favor of a mutually beneficial policy of the Middle Way, and we have made sincere, persistent efforts to put it into practice for several years now.

Since 2002, my envoys have conducted six negotiation sessions with their counterparts in the People's Republic of China to approach these important problems. These exhaustive discussions helped appease certain doubts and helped us explain our aspirations. However, when it comes down to it, there has been no concrete result. During these last few years, Tibet has experienced an increase of brutal repression. Despite these unfortunate events, my determination and my commitment to pursuing the policy of the Middle Way and conducting dialogues with the Chinese government remain unchanged.

One major concern of the People's Republic of China is its lack of legitimacy in Tibet. The best method that the Chinese government could use to strengthen its position would be to pursue a policy that could satisfy the Tibetan people and win its trust. If we are able to reconcile with the Chinese by coming to an agreement, then, as I have stated many times, I will try to win the support of the Tibetan people for it.

In Tibet at present, because of numerous actions carried out without any foresight on the part of the Chinese government, the natural environment is severely damaged. Moreover, because of the policy of demographic transfer, the non-Tibetan population has increased massively, reducing native Tibetans to an insignificant minority in their own country. What's more, the language, customs, and traditions of Tibet, which reflect the true nature and identity of our people, are in the process of disappearing. The result is that Tibetans find themselves progressively assimilated into the more numerous Chinese population.

In Tibet, repression continues to be exercised with numerous, flagrant, unimaginable violations of human rights, denial of religious freedom, and the politicization of religion. All this stems from the Chinese government's lack of respect for the Tibetan people. These are major obstacles that the Chinese government is deliberately setting in the way of its policy of unifying nationalities. These obstacles separate Tibetans from Chinese. That is why I call on the Chinese government to put an immediate end to this policy.

Although the zones inhabited by the Tibetan population are labeled by the names of autonomous regions, autonomous prefectures and autonomous counties, they are autonomous in name only and in reality do not enjoy any autonomy whatsoever. On the contrary, they are governed by people who are ignorant of the regional situation and dominated by what Mao Zedong called "Han chauvinism." In fact, the so-called autonomy has not given any tangible benefits to the nationalities concerned. These mistaken policies, which are not in keeping with reality, cause enormous damage, not only to the different nationalities, but also to the unity and stability of the Chinese nation. It is important for the Chinese government to follow the advice given by Deng Xiaoping: "look for the truth based on the facts," in the literal sense.

The Chinese government severely criticizes me when I raise the question of the welfare of the Tibetan people before the international community. Until we manage to find a mutually beneficial solution, I have the moral and historical responsibility to continue to speak freely in the name of all Tibetans. In any case, everyone knows that I have been in semi-retreat since the new political leadership of the Tibetan diaspora was elected by the people.

China is developing and is becoming a powerful country thanks to major economic progress. We welcome this with a positive mind, all the more so since it is a chance for China to play an important role on a global level. The world waits with impatience to see how Chinese leadership today will apply its concepts of "harmonious society" and "peaceful growth" that it advocates. In this domain, economic development will not be enough by itself. There must be progress in respect for the law, in transparency, and in freedom of information and expression. Since China is a country of many nationalities, they should all enjoy equal rights and the freedom to protect their respective identities. That is a condition for the stability of the country.

On March 6, 2008, President Hu Jintao declared, "The stability of Tibet concerns the stability of the country, and the security of Tibet concerns the security of the country." He added that the Chinese government should ensure the wellbeing of Tibetans and improve its actions toward religious and ethnic groups, while maintaining social harmony and stability. President Hu Jintao's statement is in keeping with reality, and we ask that it be applied.

In 2008, the Chinese people proudly and impatiently awaited the opening of the Olympic Games. From the beginning, I supported the idea that China should host the Olympic Games. Since such international sporting events, the Olympics especially, bring the principles of freedom of expression, equality and friendship to the fore, China should demonstrate the quality of its welcome by granting these freedoms. In sending its athletes, I felt the international community should remind China of its duties. Several parliaments, individuals, and nongovernmental organizations throughout the world took numerous initiatives, stressing the chance this opportunity gave

China to initiate a positive change. The Olympic Games undoubtedly had a great impact on the minds of everyone in the Chinese community. So the world should look for ways to act energetically in favor of positive changes in China, even after the end of the Games.

I would like to express my pride in and approval of the sincerity, courage, and determination the Tibetan people in Tibet have shown. I actively encourage Tibetans to continue to work peacefully, respecting the law. I urge that all national minorities in the People's Republic of China, including the Tibetan people, be able to enjoy their legitimate rights.

I would also like to thank the government and people of India in particular for their continued and unparalleled aid to Tibetan refugees and to the cause of Tibet, and to express my gratitude for all the governments and all the peoples who continue to support our cause.

With my prayers for the well-being of all sentient beings.[28]

The problems expounded in this speech on March 10, 2008, are the same ones that the Dalai Lama had continued to denounce since the beginning of the Chinese occupation of Tibet. They have gotten dangerously worse over the years, and despite the support of international public opinion, the systematic tightening of Chinese control has not stopped.

A wish for dialogue and negotiation has been clearly expressed by the Dalai Lama on numerous occasions—such as in a speech during a trip to Taiwan in February 1997, when he asserted that "the Tibetans' struggle is directed not against the Chinese or China, but in an authentic spirit of reconciliation and compromise."

China responded to these statements by issuing a call to fight by every means possible "the international campaign of the Dalai clique." During a visit to the United States six months later, in October 1997, the Chinese president, Jiang Zemin, declared at Harvard: "The Dalai Lama should publicly admit that Tibet is an inalienable part of the People's Republic of China, and he should renounce the independence of Tibet and stop all activities aimed at separating it from the motherland."

Two years later, in 1999, during a state visit to France, the Chinese president repeated these statements, adding that the Dalai Lama should also admit that Taiwan was "a Chinese province." And during his yearly message on March 10 of that same year, the spiritual leader of the Tibetans declared that China had hardened its position on entering into discussions with him.

If, in order to go forward in dialogue, the Dalai Lama has many times since 1987 expressed his willingness to renounce the independence of Tibet in favor of a status of real autonomy within contemporary China, this does not mean that he is willing to rewrite his country's history and endorse the lie that Tibet is an ancient Chinese province.

International public opinion—expressed at the highest level by the moral authority of the Nobel Peace Prize—has continuously urged China to accept the hand held out by the Dalai Lama, but this pressure has only provoked Chinese officials, who express their increasing exasperation by an ever more severe repression in Tibet. The Sino-Tibetan dialogue was interrupted in 1993 and did not resume until 2002, when a delegation of the Dalai Lama's went to China and Tibet with the goal of reestablishing direct contact. Thereafter, a more profound exchange between the two parties did not happen until 2004.

In his official speech on March 10, 2005, the Dalai Lama declared, "I would once again like to reassure the Chinese authorities: as long as I am responsible for Tibetan affairs, we will remain fully committed to the Middle Way, which does not claim independence for Tibet." The Dalai Lama expressed his optimism for the gradual improvement of exchanges between his emissaries and their Chinese counterparts.

In July 2005, a meeting at the Chinese embassy in Berne, Switzerland, aroused much hope when Chinese delegates assured Tibetans that the Communist Party would accord "very great importance to relations with the Dalai Lama." Then, in February 2006 and again in July 2007, during new meetings in Beijing, both parties declared that they had reviewed the conditions necessary to resolve their differences. The Tibetan emissaries insisted on the urgency of dealing with fundamental questions, while expressing the Dalai Lama's wish to make a pilgrimage to China.

These negotiations were the longest and most promising ever undertaken. That is why, in his speech on March 10, 2008, while he regretted that the discussions had not yet resulted in concrete actions and that Beijing was persisting in its demographic aggression and its violation of human rights in Tibet, the Dalai Lama was pleased with President Hu Jintao's declaration affirming that the Chinese government would ensure "the well-being of Tibetans and improve its actions toward religious and ethnic groups, while maintaining social harmony and stability."

But in the days that followed, Lhasa rose up in revolt.

In China, I see that change
is on the way

SEVERAL DISTINGUISHED members of the European Parliament are well aware of my continued efforts to find a mutually agreeable solution to the Tibetan problem through dialogue and negotiation. It was in this spirit that, in 1988, at the European Parliament of Strasbourg, I presented a proposal in due form for negotiations that did not call for the separation or independence of Tibet. Since then, our relations with the Chinese government have experienced many highs and lows. After an interruption of almost ten years, in 2002 we reestablished direct contacts with the Chinese government.

Exhaustive discussion has taken place between my emissaries and representatives of the Chinese regime. In these negotiations, we clearly presented the aspirations of the Tibetan people. The essence of my Middle Way policy is to guarantee an authentic autonomy for our people within the constitution of the People's Republic of China.

During the seventh cycle of meetings in Beijing, on July 1 and 2, 2008, the Chinese party invited us to present our point of view on the form that an authentic autonomy should take. Consequently, on October 31, 2008, we presented to the Chinese government the "memorandum on the true autonomy of the Tibetan people." This text set forth our position on what an authentic autonomy would be and explained how to satisfy the basic needs of the Tibetan nation to arrive at autonomy and self-determination. We listed these suggestions with the sole aim of making a sincere effort to solve the real problems in Tibet. We were confident that, with goodwill, the questions raised in our memorandum could be resolved.

Unfortunately, the Chinese party rejected it in its totality, declaring that our suggestions were an attempt to regain a "semi-independence" and that it was a matter of a "disguised independence," which, for that reason, was unacceptable. What's more, the Chinese party accused us of "ethnic cleansing" under the pretext that our memorandum called for a recognition of the right of autonomous regions "to regulate the residence, settlement and employment or economic activities of persons coming from other parts of the People's Republic of China wanting to settle in Tibet."

We clearly expressed that our intention was not to expel non-Tibetans. Our concern was the increasing transfer of settlements, mainly Hans, to many Tibetan regions, which marginalizes the native Tibetan population and threatens the fragile ecosystem of Tibet. Major demographic changes, resulting from massive immigration, will lead to the assimilation rather than to the integration of Tibetan identity in the People's Republic of China and will gradually lead to the extinction of the distinct culture and identity of the Tibetan people.

While firmly rejecting the use of violence to lead our struggle, I affirm that we certainly have the right to explore all other possible political options. In a democratic spirit, I called for a special meeting of Tibetans in exile to debate the status of the Tibetan people and the future of our movement. The meeting took place from November 17 to 22, 2008, in Dharamsala, India. The failure of the Chinese government to respond favorably to our initiatives revived the suspicions of many Tibetans who thought that the Chinese government was not interested in any mutually acceptable solution whatsoever. Many Tibetans continue to believe that the Chinese regime is only envisaging a complete, forced assimilation and absorption of Tibet by China, so they call for the complete independence of Tibet. Others advocate the right to self-determination and ask for a referendum on Tibet. Despite these different points of view, the delegates at our special meeting unanimously resolved to give me full power to decide on the best possible approach, keeping in mind the present situation and the changes in Tibet, in China, and throughout the world.

I have always argued that in the end it is the Tibetan people who should decide on the future of Tibet. As Pandit Nehru, who was prime minister of India, declared before the Indian Parliament on December 7, 1950: "The final word on Tibet should be given by the Tibetan people and no one else."

The cause of Tibet has a dimension and implication that go beyond the fate of six million Tibetans. It also concerns over thirteen million people living throughout the Himalayas, Mongolia, and the Kalmuk and Buriat Republics in Russia, as well as a growing number of our Chinese brothers and sisters who share our Buddhist culture, which is capable of contributing to the peace and harmony of the world.[29]

The Dalai Lama gave this speech at the European Parliament in Brussels in December 2008, after the mass uprisings that agitated Tibet starting on March 10 of China's Olympic year, after the demonstrations that took place during the passing of the Olympic torch through the world's capitals. Chinese repression was brutal, blind, and thorough. Rumor has it that there were so many arrests that the Chinese police ran out of handcuffs and had to tie prisoners up with cables.

On March 14, Zhang Qingli, secretary of the Communist Party for the autonomous region of Tibet, described the situation in Lhasa as a "fight to the death" against the Tibetan separatists. At a meeting with the heads of the People's Armed Police, he expressed his pleasure that the March demonstrations allowed them to "test their ability to respond to an emergency in case of riots."

The number of victims has not yet been verified, since there are still more than one thousand people missing. And information is filtered, since all communications are censored—to such an extent that even many months afterward, Tibetans in India have told us that they were not phoning their families out of fear of endangering them.

We now know that thousands of Tibetans—monks, nuns, laypeople, old people, and even children—were arrested. Over 200 were condemned, and at least 150 died, sometimes under torture and beatings. Some spoke of a "second Cultural Revolution" given the methods used by the Chinese regime following the closing of hundreds of monasteries throughout the country. Monastic compounds in the Lhasa valley were besieged by armored tanks for weeks, and laypeople were dissuaded from bringing in food or water. At least one monk is said to have died of hunger in Ramoche monastery. Once again people witnessed the pillaging of valuable religious objects, and meetings of "patriotic reeducation" were organized to force ordained people to deny the Dalai Lama in writing, under penalty of being accused of separatism and imprisoned.

Chinese propaganda accused the spiritual leader in exile of fomenting these revolts, calling him a "criminal," a "traitor to the homeland," and a "separatist," while Zhang Qingli called him a "wolf with a man's face but an animal's heart." To these insults, the Dalai Lama replied humorously that he would willingly submit to a blood test to determine whether he is man or animal. But more seriously, he deplored the serious attack on human rights when the Chinese authorities forced ordained people to insult him and, under threat, deny him.

The Dalai Lama received the first reports and images of atrocities committed by the Chinese authorities when he was with Samdhong Rinpoche.

He remembers that their eyes filled with tears and that he felt overwhelmed by the suffering: "I was simply sad, profoundly sad," he said.

In early January 2009, during a teaching in Sarnath, India, he declared that he had meditated on the prayer of the great Indian sage Shantideva, which speaks of an enemy as the best teacher, since he forces us to develop patience and deepen our tolerance and forgiveness. To a journalist who asked him if he had felt anger, the Dalai Lama replied that anger was foreign to him, since this emotion means that one wants to harm someone: "My faith helps me overcome this negative emotion and keep my equilibrium. Each of my Buddhist rituals is part of a process where I give and receive. I receive Chinese mistrust and I send compassion. I pray for the Chinese, for their leaders, and even for those who have blood on their hands."[30]

The Dalai Lama's analysis of the explosive situation is lucid. He notes that oppression and torture have not succeeded at politically "reeducating" the Tibetans. To offset the controversy aroused by the massive settlement of Han Chinese, the leaders of the Chinese Communist Party put into effect several programs to improve the quality of life, injecting billions of yuan into huge infrastructure projects. But in the eyes of the Tibetans, the most important thing is to recover their basic liberties along with their cultural identity and scorned spirituality.

In December 2008, at the European Parliament, the Dalai Lama reasserted the pertinence of his Middle Way policy, with its goal of ensuring general autonomy and guaranteeing Tibetans the right to settle questions of a cultural, religious, or environmental order themselves. There is no question of the country's independence since, from the standpoint of international law, Tibet would be integrated into the People's Republic of China, which would remain in charge of foreign relations and defense.

The Middle Way policy, however, has been the subject of increasingly virulent debate, especially on the part of the young members of the Tibetan Youth Congress—a "terrorist" organization, according to the Chinese Communist Party—whose members call for independence. The Dalai Lama himself admits that the Middle Way policy has not produced any of the hoped-for results. The poet Tenzin Tsendu comments on the reasons for this failure: "The Dalai Lama had based himself on the conviction that the Chinese leaders were also human beings, capable of sitting around a table and discussing things. But in spite of persisting for years in searching for a compromise, maintaining dialogue throughout and despite everything, in spite of a sincere effort to humanize relations, this dialogue has not succeeded. The Dalai Lama recognizes that China is not playing the game."[31]

Thus, at the European Parliament meeting at the end of 2008, the Dalai Lama did not rule out the possibility of abandoning the proposal for autonomy and going back to calling for independence. But he also admitted that he could not discount the possibility of a final solution for Tibet: to keep control over Tibet, a country rich in natural resources, the Chinese leaders might oppress the population ever more brutally and use increases in demographic transfers of Chinese settlements to make the Tibetans once and for all into an insignificant minority in a Tibet populated by the Hans.

Although this scenario cannot be ruled out, a new element feeds the Dalai Lama's hope: the evolution of the Chinese people, and the Dharma connections that have developed in recent decades. After congratulating the European deputies on the awarding of the Sakharov Human Rights Prize to Hu Jia, the spiritual leader asserted that even if he could no longer believe in the declarations of the Chinese government, his confidence in the Chinese people remained "intact."

To all my spiritual brothers
and sisters in China

I WOULD LIKE TO APPEAL PERSONALLY to all my spiritual brothers and sisters in China, both inside and outside the People's Republic, especially to the disciples of the Buddha. I speak as a Buddhist monk and a student of our revered teacher, the Buddha. I have already appealed to the Chinese community in general, but this time you are the ones I am addressing, my spiritual brothers and sisters, on the subject of an urgent humanitarian question.

The Chinese and Tibetan peoples share a common spiritual heritage in Mahayana Buddhism. We venerate the Buddha of Compassion—Guan Yin in the Chinese tradition and Chenrezig in the Tibetan tradition. We cherish as the highest spiritual ideal compassion for all beings suffering. Given that Buddhism flourished in China before it was transmitted from India to Tibet, I have always regarded Chinese Buddhists with the respect due to spiritual older brothers and sisters.

As most of you know, beginning on March 10, 2008, a series of demonstrations took place in Lhasa and several other regions in Tibet. These events were provoked by profound Tibetan resentment of the policies of the Chinese government. I was very saddened by the losses of human life, on both sides, Chinese and Tibetan, and I immediately asked for restraint on the part of both the Chinese authorities and the Tibetans. I especially asked the Tibetans not to resort to violence.

Unfortunately, the Chinese authorities used brutal methods to check the revolt despite appeals from numerous heads of state, NGOs [nongovernmental organizations], and world-famous individuals, especially many Chinese scholars. In the course of these events, some people lost their lives, others were wounded, and a large number were imprisoned. The attacks continued, and it aimed especially at the institution of monasticism, where the traditions of our ancestral Buddhist wisdom are preserved. Over the years of my exile, many monasteries have been closed. We have received reports telling of imprisoned monks being beaten and treated cruelly. These repressive measures seem to be part of a policy of systematic, officially approved sanctions.

Without international observers, journalists, or even tourists authorized to enter Tibet, I am deeply worried about the fate of the Tibetans. Many wounded people, victims of repression, especially in remote regions, are too afraid of being arrested ever to ask for medical care. According to trustworthy sources, people are fleeing into the mountains, where they have access to neither food nor shelter. Those who remain are living in a permanent state of fear, afraid of being arrested.

I am extremely disturbed by these continued sufferings. My concern is extreme, and I wonder what the result of all these tragic developments will be. I do not believe that repression is a viable solution in the long run. The best way to go forward is to resolve the questions concerning Tibetans and Chinese through dialogue, and I have defended this position for a long time. In recent years I have often assured the government of the People's Republic of China that I am not asking for independence. What I am looking for is a significant autonomy for the Tibetan people, capable of guaranteeing the long-term survival of our Buddhist culture, our language, and our distinct identity. The rich Tibetan culture is part of the general cultural heritage of the People's Republic of China, and it can be beneficial for our Chinese brothers and sisters.[32]

It was in the United States at the end of April 2008, during his first trip abroad after the general uprising in Tibet, that the Dalai Lama launched an appeal to the Chinese. In a speech to the Asian community, he reviewed the history of his attempts at a negotiated solution for Tibet, affirming his sincerity and openness, while deploring the absence of response on the part of the Beijing authorities.

In this second speech to the Buddhist Chinese, the tone is more personal. The Dalai Lama addresses his "brothers and sisters"; coming from him, these words are not without meaning. This fraternal link exists on the human, historic, and spiritual levels, for all Buddhists are disciples of the same teacher, Buddha Shakyamuni. In 2008 the Dalai Lama appealed to a rediscovered fraternity around an ideal of freedom and democracy. And his statements have echoed in the People's Republic, which is not really monolithic. In 1996 the dissident Liu Xiabo was condemned to three years in a concentration camp for writing a letter to President Jiang Zemin calling for self-determination for the Tibetans and an opening of dialogue with the Dalai Lama.

In Chinese society today, journalists, lawyers, ecologists, and artists have the courage to confront the authorities. As it undergoes major change, China is rediscovering religion. According to the Tibetan prime minister, Samdhong Rinpoche, there are 300 million Buddhists in China, including the ex-leader of the Communist Party, Jiang Zemin, and the former prime minister, Zhu Rongji. Many businessmen and artists are interested in Buddhism, and books by the Dalai Lama, printed in Taiwan, circulate under cover. While sympathy for and solidarity with the Tibetan cause continue to increase, rich benefactors have financed the reconstruction, in the great Tibetan tradition, of destroyed monasteries and centers of transmission of the Buddha's teaching.

The Dalai Lama maintains hope for an eventual democratization of China and for justice that would be rendered to the Tibetans by the Chinese people.

The Dalai Lama wonders, "What if spirituality were to overthrow Chinese communism?" He has asked the question many times, for this hypothesis does not seem unlikely to him. It is inscribed in the logic of the spiritual revolution that he advocates and in his three commitments in life. If his work in the service of freedom and peace throughout the world is not finished, his next incarnation, the fifteenth in the line of Dalai Lamas, will take up the torch of freedom, which is not even close to going out—it burns in the heart of a human being whose life does not end with death.

I Place My Hope in the Human Heart

We Can Only Live in Hope

IN SPITE OF THE ATROCIOUS CRIMES the Chinese have committed in our country, I have absolutely no hatred in my heart for the Chinese people. I believe that one of the curses and dangers of the present age is to blame nations for the crimes of individuals. I have known many admirable Chinese.

In these days of overwhelming military power all men and women can only live in hope. If they are blessed with peaceful homes and families, they hope to be permitted to keep them and to see their children grow up in happiness; if they have lost their homes, as we have, their need for hope and faith is even greater. The hope of all men, in the last analysis, is simply for peace of mind. My hope rests in the courage of Tibetans and the love of truth and justice that is still in the heart of the human race, and my faith is in the compassion of Lord Buddha.[33]

BE A SOURCE OF HOPE!

Whatever happens
Never lose hope!
Develop your heart.
In your country, too much energy
Is devoted to cultivating the mind.

Be a source of compassion,
Not just for your friends,
But for everyone.
Be a source of compassion.
Work for peace.
And I tell you again,
Never lose hope,
Whatever happens,
Whatever happens around you
Never lose hope!

This poem was written by the Dalai Lama at the request of the American writer Ron Whitehead, founder of a medical research institute studying the human genome. The Dalai Lama read it at New York University in April 1994 during a festival organized by Ron Whitehead dedicated to world peace.

"Never lose hope," a slogan taken up by Tibetan youth, is now inscribed on houses in children's villages and printed on T-shirts.

MAY I REMAIN IN ORDER TO RELIEVE THE SUFFERINGS OF THE WORLD!

May I be the protector of the abandoned,
The guide for those who wander the path,
And for those who yearn for the other shore,
May I be the vessel, the ferry, the bridge;
May I be the island for those who need an island,
The lamp for those who need a lamp,
The bed for those who need a bed;

May I be the wish-fulfilling gem, the vase
With great treasure, a powerful mantra, the healing plant,
The wish-granting tree, the cow of abundance.
As long as space remains,
As long as beings remain
May I too remain
To relieve the sufferings of the world![34]

It was with this last quatrain of the long prayer by the great Indian saint Shantideva, which exalts the Buddha's love for all sentient beings, that the Dalai Lama concluded his speech accepting the Nobel Peace Prize in 1989.

Almost twenty years later,[35] he confided that at the time of his death he wants to leave this life remembering these lines, his mind bathed in compassion.

AFTERWORD

Winning Peace with the Dalai Lama

On the occasion of the fiftieth anniversary of the Dalai Lama's exile, this book would like to celebrate a victory.

In the history books we learn that one nation wins a war while another loses it. Over the centuries, conflicts have succeeded each other, showing how true it is that no war that has ever been won has signified the end of war. Quite the contrary. Confrontation continues from generation to generation, and the parties that capitulated yesterday hope to become the conquerors of tomorrow. What if the Dalai Lama's commitment were precisely to break this cycle of conflict? From that point of view, the fifty years that have passed would be neither pointless nor lost. On the contrary, they would represent victory over war.

The Dalai Lama has won peace; he has come away with a victory of peace.

This victory is not proclaimed on the front pages of newspapers, and nations have not given a triumphant welcome to the man who won this battle, taking as his inspiration and political model Mahatma Gandhi. The battle waged by the Dalai Lama cannot be seen as similar to the thousands of bombs raining down on populations taken hostage by clashes between governments. His battle cannot be heard like the explosions resounding through what is usually called the "theater" of military operations. But a battle has been waged and continues to be waged by the spiritual leader of the Tibetans, according to the rules of a determined strategy of nonviolence, with unflagging perseverance.

In this combat, the enemy is not who one might think it is. The Dalai Lama is not fighting against the Chinese. How could he call the Chinese his enemies? When he speaks of them, he has for many years called them his "brothers and sisters." An advocate of both inner and outer disarmament, he advances onto the international scene with bare hands. No terrorist, no planter of bombs, no kamikaze cites the Dalai Lama as his inspiration. To the younger generation of Tibetans who want to fight with the Chinese occupier, he insists on the path of nonviolence, from which he has never strayed.

When he left Tibet in 1959, the Dalai Lama could not carry any wealth with him; that was the price of his successful flight beyond the Himalayan barrier. But this does not mean that he was destitute. Stripped of material goods, he carried within himself the treasures of wisdom, love, and compassion he had cultivated since childhood. In the Potala monastery, in the secrecy of its age-old walls, he had practiced handling the weapons that defeat all weapons, weapons that prepare for the victory of peace.

The military occupation of Tibet by the Chinese nation, the violation of human rights, the forced sinicization of the inhabitants, and the demographic aggression are flagrant, painful, and unbearable. The Dalai Lama has ceaselessly denounced them for over fifty years to the community of nations, whose response has not matched the gravity of events on the Roof of the World. The recognition of the

Tibetan genocide by the International Commission of Jurists in 1950 led to no measures against China. And although the Dalai Lama has managed to mobilize public opinion throughout the world, he has not obtained a commitment from the community of nations capable of stopping the violation of human rights in Tibet. Does this mean that love and compassion are powerless against China's economic interests and the force of massive blows by the Chinese government? One might think so at first, and one might wax ironic about the idealism of the leader of the Tibetans, a monk who represents the last theocracy of another age, which he transformed into a democracy in the first years of his exile. But another interpretation soon emerges.

For half a century, the Dalai Lama has appealed to the world's conscience. At a time of global society and history, when human rights are flouted in Tibet, isn't it the humanity of all of us that is violated? The victory of peace over a dictatorship that does not respect the Universal Declaration of Human Rights can only be a victory for everyone.

What if, in order to transform the world, we have to begin by transforming ourselves? By assuming our universal responsibility? What if, following the Dalai Lama's example, we were all called on to become "peacemakers" in order to liberate ourselves by liberating six million Tibetans, thus leaving future generations with a more human, more fraternal world?

We must come to some sort of realization now, so that we are not destroyed by remorse for having been passive witnesses of a tragedy and so that, with the Dalai Lama, we can win peace.

—Sofia Stril-Rever
Kirti Monastery
Dharamsala, December 2008

NOTES

Foreword

1. The first Dalai Lama, venerated as an emanation of Avalokiteshvara, the Buddha of Compassion, lived from 1391 to 1474.

2. *Dalaï-lama, une vie après l'autre:* a documentary directed by Franck Sanson, based on an idea by Mehramouz Mahvash, and written by Sofia Stril-Rever.

My Three Commitments in Life

1. Speech delivered to the European Parliament, Brussels, December 4, 2008.

Part One: As a Human Being

1. Acceptance speech for the Congressional Gold Medal, Washington, D.C., October 17, 2007.

2. "Human Rights, Democracy, and Freedom," statement for the sixtieth anniversary of the Universal Declaration of Human Rights, December 10, 2008.

3. Nobel Peace Prize acceptance speech, Oslo, December 10, 1989.

4. Statement made in Taiwan, June 2008.

5. See Paul Ekman, ed., *Emotional Awareness: Overcoming the Obstacles to Psychological Balance and Compassion* (New York: Times Books, 2008).

6. A *dzomo* is a cross between a yak and a cow.

7. Heinrich Harrer, *Seven Years in Tibet,* trans. Richard Graves (London: R. Hart-Davis, 1953), p. 225.

8. Statement by the Dalai Lama in Amaravati, January 10, 2006.

9. *Dharma* is a polysemous Sanskrit word meaning, here, "the teaching of the Buddha."

10. Gendun Drupba, the first Dalai Lama, lived for eighty-three years.

11. Samdhong Rinpoche is Kalon Tripa, or prime minister, of the Tibetan government in exile. Born in Kham in 1939, he was recognized as a reincarnate lama at the age of five, and he went into exile in India, following the Dalai Lama, in 1959. In 2001 he was elected Kalon Tripa for the first time, with 84.5 percent of the vote.

12. Declaration made on December 2, 2007.

13. Shantarakshita, an eighth-century spiritual master and Indian philosopher, introduced Buddhism to Tibet at the invitation of King Trisongdetsen.

14. The Tibetan term *tulku,* which designates lamas who are leaders of their lineage, is the translation of the Sanskrit *nirmanakaya,* which means "transformation body."

15. The Fourteenth Dalai Lama, interview with Martin Brauen, in *The Dalai Lamas: A Visual History* (Zurich: Serindia Publications, 2005), 9–10.

16. Quoted in Claude B. Levenson, "Tibet, le talon d'Achille de Pékin (Tibet, Beijing's Achilles' Heel)," *Revue de politique internationale* 117 (Fall 2007).

17. Egil Aarvik, speech presenting the Nobel Peace Prize, Oslo, December 10, 1989.

18. The Dalai Lama and Victor Chan, *The Wisdom of Forgiveness: Intimate Conversations and Journeys* (New York: Penguin, 2004), 14.

Part Two: As a Buddhist Monk

1. Excerpted from the Dalai Lama, *The Good Heart: A Buddhist Perspective on the Teachings of Jesus,* edited by Robert Kiely (Boston: Wisdom Publications, 1998), 38–42.

2. The Sanskrit word *mara* can be translated as "demon."

3. Aryadeva, an Indian sage of the second and third centuries, was the principal disciple of Nagarjuna, the author of fundamental Buddhist treatises.

4. The "essences" are the elements of the subtle body.

5. Tsongkhapa, a Tibetan saint and scholar of the thirteenth century, founded the Gelugpa school, to which the institution of the Dalai Lamas belongs.

6. Lama Thubten Yeshe, *Introduction to Tantra: The Transformation of Desire,* edited by Jonathan Landaw (Boston: Wisdom Publications, 2001), 32–33.

7. The September 11, 2001, attacks.

8. Speech to the European Parliament, Strasbourg, October 14, 2001.

9. "Human Rights, Democracy, and Freedom," speech given in Dharamsala, 2008.

10. Excerpt from a speech to the Society for Neurosciences, Washington, DC, November 12, 2005.

11. Ibid.

12. Nagarjuna, "Hymn to the Buddha Who Transcends the World" (in Sanskrit, *Lokatishtava;* in Tibetan, *'Jig rten las 'das par bstod pa*).

13. Speech delivered January 14, 2003.

14. His Holiness the Dalai Lama, *Ancient Wisdom, Modern World: Ethics for a New Millennium* (New York: Little, Brown and Co., 1999), 214–16.

15. Excerpt from a speech given at the "Tibet in Danger" conference, Sydney, Australia, September 28, 1996.

16. In this epithet for the Buddha, *Tathagata* is the Sanskrit term for "thus-gone."

17. Ikshvaku is the first king of the solar dynasty of Ayodhya, the origin of the Chakravartin lineage, into which Prince Siddhartha Gautama, who became the historical Buddha Shakyamuni, was born.

18. Avalokiteshvara is the Sanskrit name (Chenrezig in Tibetan) for the Buddha of Compassion.

19. The Tantras are the treatises of Vajrayana Buddhism that describe the subtle body.

20. Tsongkhapa (1357–1419), great teacher of Tibetan Buddhism. He recast the Kadampa tradition and renewed it, establishing Ganden Monastery, where the new Gelukpa school originated. The Dalai Lama is the most notable figure in the Gelukpa tradition. Manjushri is the meditation deity who embodies wisdom and learning.

21. *Vinaya* is the Sanskrit term for "monastic discipline."

22. The Kalpataru is one of the five trees of Svarga, the heaven of the god Indra, situated at the top of Mount Meru, where the souls of mortals migrate after living virtuously and stay until the time comes for them to resume an earthly body. Legend says that the Kalpataru grants all wishes.

23. The Jambu tree, or rose apple tree, gives its name to Jambudvipa, the southern continent, the one inhabited by human beings according to the Buddhist cosmology of the Abhidharma.

24. To avoid destroying insects and earthworms when the foundations were built.

25. Poem written to accompany the offering made by the Dalai Lama of a statue of the Buddha to the Indian people during the opening of the "International Conference on Ecological Responsibility," New Delhi, October 2, 1993.

26. The Buddha was born in Lumbini, Nepal, near the village of Kapilavastu.

27. It was as he sat at the foot of the Bodhi Tree—which was a pipal tree (*Ficus religiosa*)—that Prince Siddhartha Gautama attained Enlightenment. In Bodhgaya, on the historic place of Enlightenment, Buddhists venerate a tree that is said to be the offshoot of the Bodhi Tree.

28. Teaching given in Sarnath, January 14, 2009.

29. This initiation in Beijing was given in 1932.

30. Quoted from the teaching given at the conclusion of the initiation on December 29, 1990. See the development of this theme in the book *Kalachakra: Un mandala pour la paix* by Sofia Stril-Rever and Mathieu Ricard, with a preface by the Dalai Lama (Paris: Éditions de la Martinière, 2008).

31. Declaration at the U.S. Environmental Protection Agency, Washington, DC, 1991.

32. Speech delivered September 20, 1991, at the inauguration of the World Conservation Union's "Take Care of the Earth" campaign, September 21, 1991.

33. Excerpt from Edmond Blattchen, *La Compassion universelle* (interviews with the Dalai Lama), translated into French by Mathieu Ricard (Liège: Alice Editions), 34.

34. Excerpt from UNESCO, "Earth Charter" (Paris: UNESCO, March 2000), available at: http://www.earthcharterinaction.org/content/pages/Read-the-Charter.html. The International Secretariat of the Earth Charter, on the campus of the University for Peace in San José, Costa Rica, coordinates global programs and projects in connection with fifty-three national committees of the Earth Charter and partner organizations such as the National Councils for Sustainable Development.

Part Three: As the Dalai Lama

1. This spiritual master–lay protector relationship is called *chö-yon* in Tibetan.

2. The Dalai Lama, *My Land and My People: Memoirs of the Dalai Lama of Tibet* (New York: Potala Corp., 1977), 75.

3. See Tibet Justice Center, "Appeal by His Holiness the Dalai Lama of Tibet to the United Nations (1950)," UN document A11549-11 (Kalimpong, November 1950), 5, available at: http://www.tibetjustice.org/materials/un/un2.html.

4. The International Commission of Jurists is the UN consulting organization that examined the Tibetan question in 1950.

5. Located on the shores of the Brahmaputra, in the Indian state of Assam, Tezpur was the first Indian town across the Indo-Tibetan border. It sheltered the Dalai Lama and his retinue for several days after their escape.

6. Mussoorie is a city in the Indian state of Uttarakhand, in the foothills of the Himalayas. In April 1959, at Nehru's invitation, the Dalai Lama established the Tibetan government in exile there, before transferring it to Dharamsala in 1960. The first Tibetan school was founded in Mussoorie in 1960; today about five thousand Tibetans live there.

7. In February 1957, Nehru had advised the Dalai Lama to negotiate the principles of the Seventeen-Point Agreement with China.

8. Talk given in Dharamsala in May 1960.

9. The government and the prime minister are now elected by the Assembly of Deputies of the Tibetan People, which, to reflect the diaspora, includes ten deputies for each of the three provinces of Greater Tibet, two deputies for each of the five main religious schools, two deputies for Europe, and one deputy for America.

10. Speech given in Washington, DC, April 1993.

11. Ibid.

12. Declaration made in Aspen, Colorado, July 2008.

13. Speech given at the Earth Summit in Rio de Janeiro, Brazil, June 6, 1992.

14. Samdhong Rinpoche, with Donovan Roebert, *Uncompromising Truth for a Compromised World* (Bloomington, IN: World Wisdom, 2006), 156–57.

15. Speech given in Dharamsala, March 10, 1961.

16. See the facsimile published in the back of this book.

17. In 1962 detachments of the People's Liberation Army invaded the Sino-Tibetan border regions and were quickly expelled.

18. Speech given in Dharamsala, March 10, 1965.

19. See the exhaustive study on the subject by Claude B. Levenson, *Tibet: l'envers du décor* (Geneva: Éditions Olizane, 1993).

20. Speech given in Dharamsala, March 10, 1967.

21. Speech given in Dharamsala, March 10, 1968.

22. Tenzin Tsendu, *Passage de la frontière,* dictated to Sofia Stril-Rever for translation and publication in French.

23. Speech given to the Human Rights Commission of the U.S. Congress, September 21, 1987.

24. Ibid.

25. Speech to the European Parliament, Strasbourg, June 15, 1988.

26. Samdhong Rinpoche, *Uncompromising Truth for a Compromised World,* 143.

27. Speech given in Dharamsala, March 10, 1990.

28. Speech given in Dharamsala, March 10, 2008.

29. Speech given at the European Parliament, Brussels, December 4, 2008.

30. Interview with the Dalai Lama, *Der Spiegel* (May 2008).

31. Interview with the Dalai Lama, *Nouvel Observateur,* December 30, 2008.

32. Speech given in Hamilton, New York, April 24, 2008.

33. The Dalai Lama, *My Land and My People,* 233–34.

34. From Shantideva's *The Way of the Bodhisattva.*

35. At a teaching given in Lisbon in September 2007, organized by the Chanteloube Center for Buddhist Studies.

BIBLIOGRAPHY

The Dalai Lama

The Universe in a Single Atom. New York: Morgan Road Books, 2005.
Ethics for the New Millennium. New York: Riverhead Books, 1999.
Freedom in Exile. New York: HarperCollins, 1990.
My Land and My People. New York: McGraw-Hill, 1962.

The Dalai Lama and Co-Authors

Emotional Awareness: Overcoming the Obstacles to Psychological Balance and Compassion, with Paul Ekman. New York: Times Books, 2008.

The Dalai Lamas: A Visual History, with Martin Brauen. Zurich: Serindia, 2005.

Journey for Peace: His Holiness the Fourteenth Dalai Lama, text by Mathieu Ricard and Christian Schmidt, photographs by Martin Brauen. Zurich: Scalo Publishers, 2005.

The Wisdom of Forgiveness, with Victor Chan. New York: Riverhead Books, 2004.

Advice on Dying and Living a Better Life, with Jeffrey Hopkins. New York: Atria Books, 2002.

The Art of Happiness, with Howard Cutler. New York: Riverhead Books, 1998.

The Good Heart: A Buddhist Perspective on the Teachings of Jesus, with Laurence Freeman, Geshe Thubten Jinpa, and Robert Kiely. Boston: Wisdom Publications, 1998.

The Power of Compassion, with Geshe Thubten Jinpa. New York: Thorsons Publishers, 1995.

A Policy of Kindness, with Sidney Piburn. Ithaca, NY: Snow Lion Publications, 1993.

Kindness, Clarity, and Insight, with Jeffrey Hopkins. Ithaca, NY: Snow Lion Publications, 1984.

Samdhong Rinpoche

Uncompromising Truth for a Compromised World, with Donovan Roebert. Bloomington, IN: World Wisdom, 2006.

Sofia Stril-Rever

Kalachakra, un mandala pour la paix, preface by the Dalai Lama, photographs by Matthieu Ricard and Manuel Bauer. Paris: La Martinière, 2008.

Traité du mandala: Tantra de Kalachakra, foreword by the Dalai Lama, unabridged text translated from the Sanskrit. Paris: Desclée de Brouwer, 2003.

Kalachakra: guide de l'initiation et du Guru Yoga, teachings by the Dalai Lama and Jhado Rinpoche. Paris: Desclée de Brouwer, 2002.

L'initiation de Kalachakra, unabridged text of the Kalachakra ritual with commentary by the Dalai Lama. Paris: Desclée de Brouwer, 2001.

Enfants du Tibet: de coeur à coeur avec Jetsun Pema et soeur Emmanuelle. Paris: Desclée de Brouwer, 2000.

Kalachakra, photo album of Namgyal monastery, preface by the Dalai Lama. Rome: Tibet Domani, 2000.

Tantra de Kalachakra: le livre du corps subtil, preface by the Dalai Lama, unabridged text translated from the Sanskrit. Paris: Desclée de Brouwer, 2000.

༄༅། །སྤྱི་ནོར་གོང་ས་སྐྱབས་མགོན་ཆེན་པོ་མཆོག་གི་སྐུ་ཕྲེང་ ༡༠༠༢ གསུམ་བཅུ་སོ་དུ་བ་དང་ ཞེས་པའི་བཅུ་ཞེ་བརྒྱད་པའི་བོ་གསུམ་སྐབ་འི་ཡོང་ཁྱབ་པ་གསུང་བ་ཞིན།

(དགས་ཉེན་གསུམ་པ།)

༄༅། །ཕྱི་ལོ་ ༡༩༥༠ རྒྱལ་ས་ཙུ་མར་བོད་མིའི་ཞི་གྱི་ལང་ཕྲན་ནས་ལོ་ ༡༡ འབོར་ཟའི་དུས་ ཚིགས་པའི་ན། ཕོས་མི་རི་གས་ཀྱི་དོན་དུ་དཀའ་དུ་གཙོ་གཉིང་མནན་དང་ལུས་སྟོག་འདོར་ར་མགས་ཚོ་ས་ར་ཅེ་ས་ དན་དང་འབྲེལ་སྟོན་འདུན་ཉིད་རྒྱ་དང་ དཉིང་དཀའ་སྐུ་སྒྲོ་བཞིན་པ་རྣམས་ལ་གཏང་ར་མི་སེས་མཚན་ སྟེད་ཀྱི་ས་འཚམས་འདི་ཡོད།

ཕྱི་ལོ་ ༡༩༣༥ ལོར་སྐུ་འབས་འི་རྒྱ་ནག་མི་དམངས་སྤྱི་མཐུན་རྒྱལ་ཁབ་ཀྱི་ཆེས་མཐའི་དྲུ་ཐེད་དང་ ཞིབ་འཇུག་གིས་རང་བཞིན་མ་ཚོ་ས་ག་གས་དོན་གཞན་པོས་མ་གས་ཀྱི་མོ་ལུ་གྱི་ལས་ནས་མཛན་ག་ཆེན་ཆོས་ རྒྱ་ཕྲོ་ས་འཆར་བའི་པོ་ལ་གི་ར་ཆེན་བོ་ལ་བཞིན་པ་རྣམས་ལ་གཏང་ར་སེ་སམས་མཚན་ ར་ཅི་ས་དན་པའི་ལས་གྲོ་ས་ས་ནང་པ་དན་རྒྱ་ནག་མི་དམངས་སྤྱི་མཐུན་རྒྱལ་ཀྱི་སྒྲ་ས་མཁའ་ཁེ་ཅང་ འཚོ་མཛ་ར་དངངས་ཚུ་བྱ་ཏེ་བ་ལ་ཉེག། གཞིན་གྱི་སྐུ་དང་དཔལ་འི་ལམ་གྱི་སྟེ་དུ་ས་གཏན་འབེལ་ས་ཕྲུན་ས་ནས་དང་ར་ བོ་ ༡༡ རིང་བོག་མཐའ་ད་པར་གསུམ་པ་ཀྱུ་ན་བོ་ད་མོ་ཚ་མ་ར་པར་རྒྱབ་བས་ན་ཉམ་ད་གུ་གས་ལག་ལ་བཟ་ར་ ལས་ཉིད། སྟེད་དུ་ས་ཆུ་ལ་གཞིན་ས་མ་བོད་མི་སད་ཚོགས་ན་དང་ བོད་ས་སྣང་སྤྱི་ནབུ་ས་ཀྱན་ཚོ་མ་ཀྱི་ ཀྱུ་སྒྲོ་ར་དུན་བོ་བ་ར་ངང་། རྒྱ་སྒྲི་ས་ཟང་ཚོ་གས་ཀྱི་སྒྲུག་མ་ལོ་ས་མཐུན་རྒྱ་སྒྲོ་ར་ ལག་བ་ཞོ་ར་ཡོད། རྒྱ་ནག་མི་དམངས་སྤྱི་མཐུན་རྒྱལ་བའི་ཀྱི་ན་ཞོ་ས་ན་ནས་ས་ར་ཕྱིང་དུ་དབང་བ་ས་གཟ་ བ་ལ་འཕུལ་ར་ས་ ས་ཚོ་ས་ལ་ན་ཡོད་ན། འདི་ཚ་ས་ནས་ཀྱ་ས་ར་ས་ས་དག་ར་ངང་ད་ཆ་ག་ག་ཚོ་འོ་ར་ནས་འོ་ར་ས་མུ་ ཕར་དུ་ས་ལམ་གྱི་ས་ཀྱུ་ས་ར་ས་འབྲོང་ས་བས་ན་ད་སྟེ་ར་བཞི་ན་པའི་ས་ར་ས་ད་ས་ཀྱི་ས་ས་ས་སེ་ས་ས་ སག་ས་བོ་ཡོ་ས་ག་ས་ག་ས་ར་ས་ས་ས་ས་ས་ཡོ་ས།

རྒྱ་བར་ཕྱི་ལོ་ ༡༠༠༡ ནས་བཟུང་བོ་ས་བའི་ཞ་ས་ག་འེ་འབྲེལ་ལ་ས་མ་བ་ས་ར་ས་གས་ད་ས་ར་ས་ ཞ་ས་ཆོ་ས་ས་ནག་མི་ད་མངས་འི་མཐུན་ས་རྒྱ་ལ་བའི་འབྲེལ་ཡོ་ས་དུ་བྱིན་ས་རྣ་ས་ར་ས་ཆ་ས་ཞ་ས་ས་ར་བཞི་ས་འབྲེ་ལ་ཡོ་ས་ ཞ་ས་ས་བྱས་ཏེ། ཕོ་ག་ས་ག་ས་ནག་ས་ག་ས་ར་ས་མ་ས་ལ་ག་ས་ལ་ས་ར་ས་ཕ་ན་ས་ཐུ་ན་ས་འ་ད་ས་ར་ས་ར་ས་ཕུ་ན་ས་ ས་འ་ ཕ་ ར་ །

THE DALAI LAMA'S ANNUAL

SPEECH TO COMMEMORATE

THE MARCH 10, 1959,

LHASA INSURRECTION

March 10, 2007

On the occasion of the 48th anniversary of the peaceful uprising of the Tibetan people in Lhasa in 1959, I pay homage to all Tibetans who have suffered and who have sacrificed their lives for the Tibetan cause. I offer my prayers for them. I also assert my solidarity with the men and women who are still suffering from repression and who are in prison now.

In 2006, we observed both positive and negative changes in the People's Republic of China. On one hand, the hard line position was intensified, notably with a campaign of vilification against us and, even more disturbing, heightened political restriction and repression in Tibet. On the other hand, in China itself, freedom of expression became visibly more widespread. In particular, Chinese intellectuals gave rise to the idea that it was necessary to develop a more meaningful society based on spiritual values. The idea that the system currently in place is unsuited to create such a society is gaining ground;

hence the development of religious faith in general, and of interest in Buddhism and Tibetan culture in particular. What's more, many people are expressing the wish that I make a pilgrimage to China and give teachings there.

President Hu Jintao's repeated call for a harmonious society is praiseworthy. The realization of such a society involves the development of trust among the people, which can only occur when freedom of expression, truth, justice, and equality reign. Therefore it is crucial that authorities at all levels not only approve these principles, but actually put them into practice.

As to our relations with China, since 1974 we realized that the opportunity to open up a dialogue with China would inevitably present itself one day or another. We have been preparing ourselves to obtain a real autonomy in which all Tibetans would be unified, as the Chinese constitution solemnly states. In 1979, Deng Xiaoping suggested that apart from independence, all other problems concerning Tibet could all be resolved through negotiation. Since that agreed with our own conception, we opted for the policy of the mutually beneficial Middle Way. Since that time, during the twenty-eight years that have ensued, we have pursued this policy with steadfastness and sincerity. It was formulated after in-depth discussions and serious analyses with the aim of serving immediate and long-term interests of both Tibetans and Chinese. It also would contribute to peaceful coexistence in Asia and to the protection of the environment. This policy was endorsed and supported by many pragmatic Tibetans both inside and outside Tibet, as well as by many nations.

The main reason behind my proposal for a genuine national regional autonomy for all Tibetans was to ensure true equality and to create a feeling of unity between Tibetans and Chinese, by eliminating both Han chauvinism and local nationalism. It would contribute to the stability of the country thanks to mutual help, trust and friendship between our two nationalities. It would also help maintain our cultural wealth and our language in proper balance between material and spiritual development, for the benefit of all humanity.

It is true that the Chinese constitution guarantees minority nationalities a national regional autonomy. The problem is that this principle is not fully put into practice. That explains why its aim, which is explicit, has not been realized: protecting the identity, culture and language of minority nationalities. What occurs on the ground is that entire populations belonging to the majority nationalities have settled in regions belonging to the minorities. Consequently, the minority nationalities, instead of being able to preserve their own identity, culture and language, have had no choice but to adopt the language and customs of the majority nationality in their own daily lives. Hence the danger of the progressive extinction of the languages and rich traditions of the minority nationalities. There is nothing inherently wrong with wanting to develop infrastructure, like railroads. Nonetheless these are the source of many problems, for since the railroad became operational, Tibet has experienced a renewed transfer of Chinese population, an acceleration of the deterioration of its environment, an increase in pollution, a mismanagement of water and exploitation of natural resources—all causes of the country's devastation and the ruin of the people living in it.

Although there are a number of educated, competent members of the Communist Party who belong to minority nationalities, it is regrettable that so few of them have obtained leadership positions on a national level. Some of them have even been accused of separatism. If we want to obtain tangible benefits for both the majority and minority nationalities, as well as for the central and regional governments, a meaningful autonomy should be established. Since this autonomy concerns minority nationalities in particular, the demand to see all Tibetans placed under one single administration is sincere, just and transparent. It is clear to the world that we have no hidden agenda. So it is a sacred duty for all Tibetans to continue the struggle until this reasonable demand is realized. It doesn't matter how long it will take; our ardor and determination will remain unchanged until the accomplishment of our aspirations. The struggle of the Tibetan people is not a fight for the special status of a few individuals; it is the struggle of an entire people. We have already transformed the Tibetan administration and community in exile into an authentically democratic structure which has seen a succession of leaders elected by the people itself. Thus we have put into place a deep-rooted, vibrant social and political institution that will continue our struggle from generation to generation. In the end, the ultimate decisions will be made democratically by the people itself.

Since the resumption of direct contact between Tibetans and Chinese in 2002, my representatives have led five rounds of comprehensive discussions with the representatives of the People's Republic of China responsible for the matter. During these discussions, both parties were able to express in clear terms the suspicions, doubts, and real difficulties that persist on both sides. These discussion sessions nevertheless helped us create a channel of communication between both parties. The Tibetan delegation stands ready to continue the dialogue at any time and any place. The Kashag (Cabinet) will give details in its own report.

I congratulate all the Tibetans in Tibet who, as members of the Communist Party, leaders, officials, professionals and others, have maintained the Tibetan spirit by conscientiously pursuing their efforts in the interest of the Tibetan people. I express my profound admiration for the Tibetans in Tibet who, despite all the challenges, have worked to preserve the Tibetan identity, culture and language. I admire their determination and unwavering courage in realizing the aspirations of the Tibetan people. I am certain they will continue to struggle for our common cause with devotion and determination. I ask all Tibetans both inside and outside Tibet to work together for a secure future based on equality and harmony between nationalities.

I would like to take this opportunity to thank the people and government of India from the bottom of my heart for their generosity and unwavering, incomparable support.

I express all my gratitude to the governments and peoples of the international community for the interest and support they bring to the Tibetan cause.

With my prayers for the peace and wellbeing of all sentient beings.

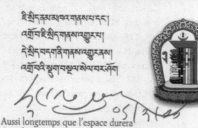

ཇི་སྲིད་ནམ་མཁའ་གནས་པ་དང་།
འགྲོ་བ་ཇི་སྲིད་གནས་གྱུར་པ།
དེ་སྲིད་བདག་ནི་གནས་གྱུར་ནས།
འགྲོ་བའི་སྡུག་བསྔལ་སེལ་བར་ཤོག

万　以　願　盡
至　及　我　除
有　眾　恆　眾
虛　生　安　生
空　住　住　苦

Aussi longtemps que l'espace durera
Aussi longtemps que les êtres demeureront
Puissé-je moi aussi demeurer
Afin de soulager les souffrances du monde

As long as space endures
As long as sentient beings remain
May I too abide
And dispel the miseries of the world

In the heart of the galaxy, the Kalachakra mandala, the Wheel of Time, is dedicated to Peace. It is inscribed in the dimension of boundless, all-encompassing love, expressed by this prayer by Shantideva, which the Dalai Lama quoted in Oslo at the end of his acceptance speech for the Nobel Peace Prize. This prayer is printed here in Tibetan, Chinese, French, and English.

The Dalai Lama's signature was affixed on February 11, 2008, in Dharamsala.

INDEX

affection, 8–10

ahimsa (nonviolent peace) zone, 224–225

altruism, 28, 29, 35–36, 102, 105–107

analysis, 88–89, 93–94, 96, 101, 121–122

anger, 21–22, 28, 129, 250

Avalokiteshvara, 7, 146, 169, 209

awareness, 77, 96–98, 101–102

"Be a Source of Hope," 259–260

Bodhi Tree, 84, 151

Border Passage (Tenzin Tsendu), 215–217

Buddha, 35, 80, 81, 84, 91, 97, 101, 127, 147–149, 151, 190, 252

Buddhism: *bodhisattva*, 65, 79; equality and freedom, 62, 190–191; impermanence, 56–57, 90–92; interdependence and compassion, 11, 158; meditation, 35–36, 77–78; nonviolence, 135, 219; other religious traditions and, 80–81; reincarnation, 55, 62–63, 65–67, 135–136; and science, 120–124, 127–131. *See also* Tibetan Buddhism; transforming the mind

Bush, George W., 192

causality, 93, 121, 152

cerebral plasticity, 122, 123

cheerfulness, 23–24

childhood development, 8–10

China, 153, 168–171, 195, 208, 220, 227–228, 233–234, 242–243, 252–254, 275–276

Chinese invasion and occupation of Tibet: attack on religion, 177, 209–211, 213, 232, 237, 249, 253; brutal repression, 202, 206–207, 228, 235–239, 248–250, 275; denouncing the Dalai Lama, 7, 181, 232, 236–237, 241, 243–244, 249; environmental degradation, 139–144, 277; genocide, 202, 264–265; Han population transfers, 208, 228–230, 238, 240, 247, 250; and India, 183–184, 207, 219, 224; initial events, 51, 165–167, 172–175, 177–179, 181–182; Lhasa insurrection, 178–179, 204, 206, 275; nuclear threat, 207, 208; ongoing flight from, 212–217; period of liberalization, 221–223; post-insurrection events in Lhasa, 197–198, 211, 232, 248–250, 252; regulatory control of lineages, 67–69; Seventeen-Point Agreement, 173, 174, 177, 183, 197; sinicization, 33, 196, 209, 211, 240–241; torture techniques, 237–238

compassion: bodhisattva ideal, 79; to heal humanity, 13, 15, 106, 112, 114, 117, 123; as path of happiness, 26–27, 88, 89, 122; practice of, 11, 18–22, 25, 28, 102; vital need for, 8–10, 14